JUVENILE DELINQUENCY, CRIME AND SOCIAL MARGINALIZATION

Social and Political Implications

JUVENILE DELINQUENCY, CRIME AND SOCIAL MARGINALIZATION

Social and Political Implications

BY

MIGUEL BASTO PEREIRA
School of Psychology, University of Minho, Portugal and Higher Institute for Applied Psychology (ISPA), Portugal

ÂNGELA DA COSTA MAIA
School of Psychology, University of Minho, Portugal

emerald
PUBLISHING

United Kingdom – North America – Japan
India – Malaysia – China

Emerald Publishing Limited
Howard House, Wagon Lane, Bingley BD16 1WA, UK

First edition 2017

British Library Cataloguing in Publication Data
A catalogue record for this book is available from the British Library

ISBN: 978-1-78743-612-1 (Print)
ISBN: 978-1-78743-611-4 (Online)
ISBN: 978-1-78743-633-6 (Epub)

Printed and bound by CPI Group (UK) Ltd, Croydon, CR0 4YY

ISOQAR certified Management System, awarded to Emerald for adherence to Environmental standard ISO 14001:2004.

Certificate Number 1985
ISO 14001

INVESTOR IN PEOPLE

CONTENTS

ACKNOWLEDGMENTS

Only a life lived for others is a life worthwhile.

— Albert Einstein

To my parents, I would like to give my sincerest gratitude, for without their constant availability and direction it would have been impossible to reach this point. To my sister, grandmother, and godmother, for their huge support and affection, I am grateful that they have been such model teachers, demonstrating how important education and knowledge is. To Catarina, I am grateful for all of the help you have given me during this journey, simplifying my life and making me happier. There are no words to express my gratitude.

To Professor David Farrington, who I met during the first year of my doctoral studies, I would like to thank for all of the great advice and support in my projects, even in those that were hardest and most ambitious, which helped me get the most of my incredible adventure at Cambridge University. To the other scholars that I met and befriended there, especially Izabela, Vicente and Maria, I am so appreciative of our conversations.

To the General Direction of the Prison Services and Probation Office, and particularly the justice professionals, it is not possible to thank you enough for your incredible and tireless support during the data collection process. To those who selflessly participated in this study and were fundamental in this scientific project, I am eternally grateful, for without you it would all have been impossible!

To Sofia Ribeiro and Ana Miranda, a special thanks for your collaboration and participation in the project of which this book is a part of. It was a sincere pleasure working with you.

I would also like to thank: Tânia Brandão and Juliana Pedro, for your longstanding friendship and for our shared love of scientific research; Rita Começanha, for your companionship and friendship, mutual cooperation and for shared experiences; Roberta, Filipe, Rui, Pedro, Cristina, Teresa, Liliana and so many other friends and colleagues who were so important to me throughout this journey.

Finally, I thank the Portuguese Foundation for Science and Technology (FCT), who financially supported my work [SFRH/BD/95190/2013], which allowed me to wrote this book. In addition, I also acknowledge that this study was conducted at Psychology Research Centre (UID/PSI/01662/2013), University of Minho, and supported by the Portuguese Foundation for Science and Technology and the Portuguese Ministry of Science, Technology and Higher Education through national funds and co-financed by FEDER through COMPETE2020 under the PT2020 Partnership Agreement (POCI-01-0145-FEDER-007653).

Miguel Basto Pereira

INTRODUCTION

Scientific evidence shows that a set of family and psychosocial elements are risk factors for juvenile delinquency. Nonetheless, a meta-synthesis of factors predicting desistance from crime in juvenile offenders, which could play a central role in preventing crime, has never been done. This is not the only limitation. If adverse childhood experiences (ACE) are a unanimous risk factor for juvenile delinquency, the role of each early adverse experience on crime and social marginalization are almost unknown. Worldwide, the levels of effectiveness of justice interventions are not encouraging, despite the majority of legal frameworks having the aim of preventing recidivism and promote social integration. Moreover, when youths with justice involvement reach adulthood, very little is known about what dimensions should be intervened.

The purpose of this book is to advance knowledge about the role of psychosocial, legal, and family factors on persistence in crime and social marginalization in young adults with a history of juvenile delinquency. This work presents the main findings and policy implications from *The Portuguese Study on Delinquency and Social Marginalization*, (PSDSM) which are divided into five parts, each part corresponding to a published and/or submitted scientific article. Chapter 1 evaluates the long-term predictors of desistance from crime in adults with a history of juvenile delinquency; Chapter 2, explores the role of adverse childhood experiences (ACE) on juvenile justice involvement, persistence in crime, and psychosocial problems; Chapter 3 examines the mechanisms involved in the link between ACE and delinquency; Chapter 4 explores the role of juvenile justice involvement and detention measures on psychosocial problems and persistence in crime during early adulthood; and, lastly, Chapter 5 evaluates the relation between adult psychosocial problems and criminal indicators in individuals with an official record of juvenile criminal offences (ORJC).

CHAPTER 1

JUVENILE DELINQUENCY, CRIME AND SOCIAL MARGINALIZATION: THEORETICAL BACKGROUND

1.1. JUVENILE DELINQUENCY: THE SCOPE OF THE PROBLEM

Juvenile delinquency is a prevalent and concerning problem. The United Nations Office on Drugs and Crime's (UNODC) most recent data from 50 countries showed that 232,041 juveniles were convicted for juvenile criminal acts in 2015 alone (UNODC, 2017). Moreover, evidence strongly suggests that the majority of individuals with adult criminal patterns had a past of juvenile delinquency (Farrington, 2003; Stouthamer-Loeber, Wei, Loeber, & Masten, 2004). However, juvenile delinquency has not only criminal implications but also relevant economic and social costs. Besides persistence in crime, several studies have shown a relationship between juvenile delinquency and school dropout (e.g., Sweeten, 2006), mental health problems (Rijo et al., 2016), drugs and alcohol misuse (Bennett, Holloway, & Farrington, 2008; Bouchery, Harwood, Sacks, Simon, & Brewer, 2011), and unemployment (Verbruggen, Blokland, & Van der Geest, 2012).

Legally, juvenile delinquency is broadly characterized as the committing of illegal acts by minors (Moeller, 2001; Regoli, Hewitt, & DeLisi, 2011). Despite this legal definition of being dependent on cultural and political backgrounds (e.g., national laws), the age of adult criminal responsibility usually ranges between 16 and 18 years in Western countries, and the majority of serious, medium, or even low-seriousness antisocial behaviors (e.g., homicide, robbery, theft, domestic violence, aggression) are criminalized worldwide (Junger-Tas & Dünkel, 2009), creating a common background for international scientific-based evidence and policies.

Criminal life careers imply an economic burden for society in general. As shown by McCollister, French, and Fang (2010) and Welsh et al. (2008), crime causes a wide range of losses affecting victims (e.g., stolen items, medical treatments, trauma), taxpayers (e.g., police, courts, prisons), and insurance companies (e.g., value-ensured stolen items, medical treatments, or mental health services costs). In addition, the criminal careers themselves have a huge long-term economic impact on the offender and society as a whole, including a higher risk of drug misuse (Bennett et al., 2008), the replacement of productive and socially relevant activities for an illegal lifestyle (McCollister et al., 2010), and a higher risk of intergenerational perpetuation of a criminal lifestyle (e.g., Day, Bevc, Theodor, Rosenthal, & Duchesne, 2008). Cohen (1998) calculated that criminal careers of juveniles aged between 14 and 17 years cost from $83,000 to $335,000 for each juvenile offender, with an additional $1.4 million being added when the juvenile criminal career persists into adulthood. More recently, Welsh et al. (2008), using the Pittsburg

Cohort, estimated that the average victim cost per juvenile chronic offender, aged between 7 and 17 years, ranged from \$793,000 to \$861,000.

Therefore, due to the tremendous tangible and intangible costs of crime, preventing and stopping juvenile delinquency and adult criminal careers and promoting social inclusion are major scientific and political aims. One of the best ways to promote these ends is using evidence-based programs and politics. However, building programs to prevent recidivism and promote social inclusion implies a deep knowledge about the mechanisms leading to juvenile delinquency and cyclically promoting criminal behavior. However, as shown by Lipsey's (2009) meta-analysis, the intervention strategies range from being harmful (e.g., deterrence) to moderately effective in reducing recidivism (e.g., counseling). In Lipsey's (2009) meta-analysis, the most effective intervention for reducing recidivism among juvenile offenders was counseling, indicating a reduction of 13% for programs with this type of intervention. Despite the fact that a reduction of 13% implies a tremendous saving on social and economic costs and even human lives, this small percentage of reduction in recidivism suggests that the majority of mechanisms promoting recidivism are not being targeted in any of the current interventions, because the mechanisms responsible are unknown or unreachable.

1.2. FACTORS PREDICTING DESISTANCE FROM CRIME IN JUVENILE OFFENDERS: SCIENTIFIC GAPS AND SCIENTIFIC EVIDENCE

Over the last two decades, important long-term longitudinal studies have been conducted to evaluate the risk factors of crime desistance in adults with a history of juvenile delinquency. The *Cambridge Study in Delinquent Development* is one of the best-known cohorts and followed 411 males, aged from 8 to 48, living in a working-class environment in South London (Farrington, Ttofi, & Coid, 2009). Out of the 411 males, 161 were convicted before the age of 20. The predictors of desistance from crime for young people between the ages of 8 and 18 were evaluated, and among several tens of variables evaluated, only hyperactivity, heavy drinking, low popularity, and harsh parental discipline negatively predicted desistance from crime in young offenders.

Likewise, the Pittsburgh Youth Study cohort followed a large sample of 850 boys from grades one, four, and seven, of whom approximately 500 were followed and evaluated at 6-month intervals (Loeber, Stouthamer-Loeber, Van Kammen, & Farrington, 1991). After 15 years, Loeber, Pardini, Stouthamer-Loeber, and Raine (2007) conducted a study analyzing risk and promotive factors of desistance from crime during late adolescence and young adulthood (17–20 years of age). Among a large range of different factors evaluated from different sources, only high interpersonal callousness, high peer delinquency, and high tobacco use negatively predicted desistance from crime and factors positively promoting desistance from crime were not found.

In addition, Moffitt (1993, 2006) theorized two typologies of youths to explain desistance from crime in juvenile delinquents: life-course-persistent trajectories versus adolescent limited. Individuals with life-course-persistent trajectories are characterized by a set of high-risk behaviors during childhood, including neuropsychological variations (e.g., cognitive deficits, hyperactivity), social and interpersonal problems (e.g., poverty, poor relations with people), and family dysfunctionality (e.g., disrupted family bounds, inadequate parenting). Those youths tend to have marginal lives, extended at least until the middle of adulthood and affecting several domains, including criminal and addictive behavior, family violence perpetration, and problems with employment.

In contrast, adolescent-limited trajectories should be more prevalent, resulting from a "maturity gap," characterized by the youngster who wants to win autonomy from their parents and take a role as an adult. Those youths are more vulnerable to mimicking their peers' delinquent lifestyle and adopting delinquent behaviors during adolescence. On entering adulthood, they usually adopt a conventional lifestyle desisting from crime. The Dunedin longitudinal study, a New Zealand cohort following 1037 boys and girls from the age of 3 until adulthood, tested this hypothesis. Twenty-three percent of the participants were classified as adolescent limited during childhood while 7% of the sample were classified as life course persistent in crime (Moffitt & Caspi, 2001). The study was conducted by Moffitt, Caspi, Harrington, and Milne (2002) when the sample reached the age of 26, and they found that children characterized as life-course persistent have higher levels of criminal convictions, including violent criminal convictions, mental health problems, substance dependence, and work problems. The analysis conducted with the Dunedin longitudinal study supports Moffitt's (2006) hypothesis to some extent, showing the relevance of this topology in explaining different trajectories. Nonetheless, it did not explain completely the phenomenon of desistance from crime as a whole, for two main reasons: (1) A significant percentage of youths classified as nondelinquent or adolescent limited also have criminal convictions and a marginal lifestyle through life; and (2) some adults classified as life-course persistent during childhood did not persist with crime or with a marginal lifestyle during adulthood.

In contrast to Terrie Moffitt, Laub and Sampson (2001) described desistance as a: "variety of complex processes — developmental, psychological, and sociological — and thus there are several factors associated with it" (p. 3), and both Kazemian (2007) and Laub and Sampson (2001) argued that, instead of a topological preselection of different trajectories, the study of desistance should include a vision of desistance as a process occurring during the lifetime, not only because the majority of criminals stop their criminal activity during their forties but also because a set of psychosocial variables during adulthood are relevant in explaining those changes in criminal careers (Sampson & Laub, 2003). In fact, while several factors are consistent in explaining juvenile delinquency (Braga, Gonçalves, Basto-Pereira, & Maia, 2017; Hawkins et al., 2000), such as abuse, neglect, drug misuse, and antisocial peers, few predictors explain desistance from crime in juvenile delinquents. In this regard, Loeber et al. (2007) concluded that both persisters and desisters were similar in a large set of psychosocial problems, including educational, employment, and substance use problems.

Nonetheless, Terrie Moffitt's work is of tremendous relevance, showing the importance of genetic and environmental factors during childhood and their predictive ability regarding persistence in crime and social marginalization. In fact, Sampson and Laub (2005) did not reject the importance of childhood experiences and characteristics on criminal behavior. Their work, using an update of Glueck's longitudinal study, with a cohort composed of 52 juvenile delinquents aged from 7 to 17 and up to 70 years, found that childhood and adolescent variables (e.g., extroversion, adventurousness, egocentricity, or violent temper tantrums) are predictors of adult crime through life. To sum up, works of Laub and Sampson (2001) and Sampson and Laub (2005) appear to suggest that childhood and adolescent factors seem to be the first step, but never the only or the last path, in understanding the process of desistance from crime.

1.3. PREVALENCE OF EARLY ADVERSE EXPERIENCES AND ASSOCIATIONS WITH PSYCHOSOCIAL DYSFUNCTION AND ANTISOCIAL BEHAVIOR

In 1998, Felitti et al. (1998) published one of the first studies to address the prevalence and correlates of childhood adverse experiences. The study, conducted in a large sample (*N* = 9508), using the Adverse Childhood Experiences (ACE) Questionnaire, addressed not only maltreatment but also a set of household dysfunctional experiences (e.g., member imprisoned, parental substance use). More than half of the participants were victims of at least one serious adverse experience and 11.1% were victims of abuse (physical and/or sexual and/or emotional abuse) in the first 18 years of life. Childhood adverse experiences were interrelated and strongly related to a set of psychosocial problems, including alcoholism, drug use, psychopathology, and adult risk behavior. Those concerning results created a new line of research and in the last 18 years a set of studies have been conducted in order to explore the prevalence and the effects of serious abuse, neglect, and household dysfunction. One of the most complete and comprehensive studies was conducted by Kessler et al. (2010) and included data from 21 countries in 5 continents (*N* = 51,945). The World Mental Health Survey was used to evaluate 12 childhood or adolescent adverse experiences. In terms of serious household dysfunction, the prevalences of parental mental illness (6.2%), parental substance disorder (4.0%), parental criminal behavior (2.9%), family violence (6.5%), parental death (12.5%), parental divorce (6.6%), other parental loss (5.1%), physical illness (3.1%), and economic adversity (3.4%) were presented. Maltreatment was also evaluated, with the most prevalent category being physical abuse (8.0%), followed by neglect (4.4%) and sexual abuse (1.6%). This study also showed that childhood adversities were strongly interrelated and associated with all classes of mental disorders during the lifetime.

More recently, the Stockholm study (Björkenstam et al., 2016) supported these findings and particularly highlighted the relevance of adversity beyond maltreatment. The study explored the role of household dysfunction in a large community sample ($N = 96{,}399$). Fifty-one percent of the sample were victims of at least one serious household dysfunction, and the cumulative exposure to childhood adversity was related to the level of utilization of psychiatric care. Likewise, Dube et al. (2003), in a study conducted in California, USA ($N = 8613$), found a relationship between drug initiation and a cumulative exposure to early adverse experiences. The prevalence of childhood adverse experiences in this sample was very high (67.3%). Moreover, more than a quarter of the sample reported having been victims of three or more serious early adverse experiences before the age of 18 (26.3%).

In Portugal, three important studies explored the prevalence and correlates of childhood adverse experiences (limited to abuse or neglect). The first study evaluated parental reports of physical and emotional abuse (Machado, Gonçalves, Matos, & Dias, 2007) in a sample of 2391 parents, with the commitment of physical abusive acts being reported by 12.3% of the parents, while 22.4% of the parents reported having been perpetrators of emotional abusive acts. Another relevant Portuguese study was conducted by Figueiredo et al. (2004) in a sample of 1000 parents. About 81.6% of parents self-reported having been victims of physical abuse and 2.6% of sexual abuse during childhood or adolescence, and this study highlighted the particularly important intergenerational role of maltreatment. In the last few years, the study conducted in Portugal by Pinto and Maia (2013) in a sample of youths with documented maltreatment found positive associations between the level of childhood adverse experiences and a set of health problems including psychopathology, physical complaints, and health risk behaviors. In addition, the study conducted by Ribeiro, Basto-Pereira, and Maia (2016) showed that youths with parents identified by the Child Protective Services (CPS) as mentally ill have almost double the prevalence of psychopathological symptoms five years later than other youths with only documented maltreatment.

In line with previous findings regarding victimization experiences (see Mesquita, Basto-Pereira, & Maia, 2017; Pinto, Correia, & Maia, 2014), the prevalence of the presence and type of childhood adverse experiences ranges from study to study, for various reasons, including differences between official documents and self-reported information, longitudinal and retrospective design, the types of surveys, and cultural differences between countries, among others. Nonetheless, the majority of studies coincide regarding the high prevalence of adverse experiences during childhood and adolescence, as well as the association between the cumulative effects of these experiences and serious long-term mental health problems.

A growing body of evidence related to adverse experiences and delinquency has been published in the last few years, particularly with regard to maltreatment. A meta-analysis conducted in 2016 by Braga et al. (2017) included 33 prospective longitudinal studies ($N = 23{,}973$ youths). This study showed maltreatment globally, and each type of maltreatment (neglect, physical, sexual, and emotional abuse) significantly predicted the risk of aggressive antisocial behavior during adolescence. The most important predictor of aggressive antisocial behavior was child sexual abuse. Nonetheless, few studies have been conducted to evaluate the impact of childhood adverse experiences beyond abuse and neglect on antisocial behavior outcomes, including juvenile delinquency and adult criminal behavior.

One of the first studies to explore the effect of other experiences beyond abuse and neglect was conducted in the United Kingdom by Roberts, Yang, Zhang, and Coid (2008) among 1396 incarcerated male offenders. This study showed that the most prevalent maltreatment experiences were parental discord (61.7%), harsh discipline at home (77.7%), and criminality of family members (55.3%), all affecting more than half of the sample. Childhood adverse experiences, such as a lack of parental affection, family substance misuse problems, parental discord, and criminality of family members, were associated with conduct disorders. In addition, all types of personality disorders showed correlations with early adverse experiences, and even more concerning was that the strongest correlation was found with antisocial personality disorder. In addition, a set of studies suggested the cross-gender, age, and cultural nature of this phenomenon. For example, in Germany, Driessen, Schroeder, Widmann, von Schonfeld, and Schneider (2006) found a high prevalence of childhood adverse experiences among incarcerated women and correlates with psychopathologic symptoms, while in Japan the same results were found in a sample of female juvenile offenders (Matsuura, Hashimoto, & Toichic, 2013).

Recently, a set of very important studies in this field were conducted by a team in Florida, USA. First, Wolff, Baglivio, and Piquero (2015) compared the prevalence of childhood adverse experiences between a large sample of juvenile offenders from the state of Florida ($N = 64{,}329$) and Felitti and Anda's Kaiser-Permanente Insured cohort, a sample of college-educated adults ($N = 17{,}337$). These authors found that juvenile offenders are 4 times more likely to score four or more different adverse experiences and 13 times less likely to score zero adverse experiences during childhood or adolescence. Baglivio and Epps (2015), using the same sample of juvenile offenders, found that the exposure to one type of adversity is strongly related to high exposure to the other types of adverse experiences. Finally, the study of Fox, Perez, Cass, Baglivio, and Epps (2015) indicated that exposure to domestic violence, emotional abuse and neglect, household substance abuse, incarcerated household member, and physical and sexual abuse during the first 18 years of life predicted violent, serious, and chronic juvenile offending when compared to juveniles with one nonviolent felony.

In Portugal, the results are in the same vein. The study conducted by Ribeiro (2015) indicated that self-reported early adverse experiences are related with self-report delinquency among youths who were identified by CPS as victims of maltreatment. Alves and Maia (2010) found a strong relationship between early adverse experiences and psychopathologic symptoms in a sample of adult female prisoners, and Alves, Dutra, and Maia (2013) study suggested that early adverse experience, risk behaviors, and psychopathology are highly prevalent among males and females prisoners.

Despite the growing number of studies in recent years, the role of each adverse experience in juvenile justice involvement and persistence in crime, and mainly in factors promoting recidivism and psychosocial problems (e.g., illegal drug use, unemployment, mental health) among individuals with history of juvenile delinquency, remains almost unexplored. One of the few efforts in the study of psychosocial problems in youth offenders, and limited to abuse and neglect, was a study conducted by Van der Put, Lanctôt, Ruiter, and Van Vugt (2015) in a sample of 13,613 juvenile offenders. The results showed that all types of maltreatment were related to all types of psychosocial problems evaluated, including alcohol abuse, drug misuse, and mental health problems.

1.4. YOUTH INVOLVEMENT IN JUVENILE JUSTICE SYSTEM: PREVALENCES AND CORRELATES WITH CRIME AND SOCIAL MARGINALIZATION

The most recent data from the United Nations Office on Drug and Crime (UNODC, 2017) from 47 countries or autonomous regions in five continents (including 25 countries from Europe) indicate that in 2015 the rate of convictions before the age of 18 ranged from 0.98 in Argentina to 441.42 in Switzerland, per 100,000 inhabitants. Among the juvenile justice measures, the rate of juvenile offenders held in prison or any penal/correctional institution ranged from 44.3 in Trinidad and Tobago, America to 0.46 in Kyrgyzstan, Asia.

Globally in 2015 alone, according to data from 56 countries, at least 28,776 youths were held in penal/ correctional institutions (UNODC, 2017). These numbers are concerning not only because juvenile delinquency is often the first step in an adult criminal career but also because we do not know the extent to which juvenile justice interventions, such as juvenile detention, are harmful or effective in different countries.

The juvenile justice measures in Portugal are served by youths aged between 12 and 20 years who have been convicted of criminal acts, committed between the ages of 12 and 15 (see Law no. 4/15; Law no. 166/99). There are eight different justice measures in Portugal, from measures served in the community to detention in juvenile justice centers, called "educational centers." According to the Ministry of Justice (DGRSP, 2016), 181 institutionalization measures in "educational centers" and 1,149 in the community were being executed at the end of 2015, mainly educational supervision, imposition of obligations (e.g., attending psychiatric treatment), community work or economic compensation and attendance at formative programs. These justice measures have the main purpose of preventing future recidivism and promoting social integration (Law no. 4/15; Law no. 166/99; Law no. 323-D/2000). In fact, globally the roots of any juvenile justice system are to avoid future criminal paths and a marginal lifestyle (Huizinga, Schumann, Ehret, & Elliott, 2003).

Despite the highest aims of juvenile justice interventions, the results from different studies are very concerning. The comparative study conducted by Huizinga et al. (2003) in the United States and German juvenile justice systems suggests that arrest and sanctioning does not fulfill its purpose in preventing recidivism, and paradoxically, in some circumstances appears to increase the risk of future criminality. In the same vein, different studies showed that juvenile justice involvement is associated with worse mental health, educational, occupational, and criminal outcomes (Gatti, Tremblay, & Vitaro, 2009; Shufelt & Cocozza, 2006; Sweeten, 2006; Tanner, Davies, & O'Grady, 1999), while the juvenile justice system more easily targets minors with specific psychological and social (e.g., low income) fragilities (Gatti et al., 2009).

These authors also highlight the fact that the impact of iatrogenic effects depends on the type of intervention. Placement in juvenile justice institutions appears to predict the worst iatrogenic effects on adult crime, after controlling for previous delinquency (Gatti et al., 2009). In this regard, Lambie and Randell (2013) summarized the current knowledge about the iatrogenic effects of juvenile detention, and these authors concluded that incarcerated youths are at greater risk of victimization, mental health problems, higher suicidal risk, and future criminal recidivism. This risk is increased in facilities with adult inmates. Exposure to criminal peers inside juvenile facilities, known as "deviant peer group contagion effects"

(Dodge, Dishion, & Lansford, 2006), as well as the exclusionary process for conventional opportunities caused by involvement in the justice system, called "labeling effects" (Bernburg & Krohn, 2003), have been pointed out as two of the most important explanations for the negative effects caused by the juvenile justice system.

Despite the negative effects caused by conventional interventions, such as incarceration or punitive sanctions, meta-analysis recently showed that treatments addressing criminogenic, family, and psychosocial needs are, in fact, effective, reducing juvenile recidivism and saving millions in costs to victims, governments, and even offenders. For example, Lipsey (2009) found that a "therapeutic" intervention philosophy (e.g., counseling, skill building) with high-risk offenders is, in fact, effective in reducing future recidivism in juvenile offenders, while discipline and a deterrence intervention philosophy increases the recidivism rates. Similarly, the meta-analysis of experimental studies on diversion programs by Schwalbe, Gearing, MacKenzie, Brewer, and Ibrahim (2012) suggests that family and restorative treatments are effective in reducing crime in juvenile offenders.

In Portugal, studies addressing the effects of juvenile justice involvement and the differential impact of each juvenile justice measure are very rare, and despite the scientific evidence provided by international meta-analytic studies regarding recidivism, globally very few studies have focused on the effect of juvenile justice measures on social (e.g., employment, school achievement), criminogenic (e.g., cognitive distortions), and psychological (mental health problems) outcomes. Nonetheless, juvenile justice measures providing better psychosocial outcomes are crucial to effectively address and stop the mechanisms promoting adult crime.

1.5. JUVENILE DELINQUENCY: WHAT PROMOTES DESISTANCE VERSUS PERSISTENCE IN CRIMINAL PATHWAYS DURING ADULTHOOD?

There is a scientific consensus that childhood and adolescent factors play a major role in subsequent criminal behavior (Farrington, in press; Moffitt, 2006). Nonetheless, when serious and recidivist juvenile delinquents reach adulthood, it is of tremendous importance to understand the factors promoting the desistance from crime. Over the last 20 years, a set of researches have been conducted to evaluate the factors promoting desistance from crime during adulthood in youths with a serious history of offending. A set of adult life events appears to reduce the odds of recidivism during adulthood and gradually promotes desistance from crime, with the most relevant events being: aging, marriage (versus separation), employment (versus unemployment), and moving home (Farrington, in press; Laub & Sampson, 2001).

Aging is probably the most important and uncontrollable factor promoting desistance from crime. Sampson and Laub (2003) conducted one of the most relevant studies exploring the impact of aging on desistance from crime using a follow-up of the 500 delinquent males from the Glueck's database. This study showed that the offending peak happens during adolescence, declines during middle adulthood, and potentially disappears during the sixties, and the authors conclude: "Aging out of crime is thus the norm — even the most serious delinquents desist" (Sampson & Laub, 2003, p. 315). Since then, other large longitudinal studies have found the same pattern (see Blonigen's, 2010 review). Neurobiological maturation processes and the effect of adult life responsibilities (such as work or marriage) have been advanced as explanations for the decrease of crime through life (Blonigen, 2010; Caspi & Roberts, 2010).

A good marriage is another life event upon which a broad consensus has built up about the effect on the reduction of offending. Sampson and Laub (1993) conducted one of the first studies in this field using the classic longitudinal data from Glueck and Glueck's. This study indicates that individuals entering a stable marriage are more likely to desist from crime. Some years later, Laub, Nagin, and Sampson (1998) established a causal relationship between a good-quality marriage and a gradual and cumulative desistance from crime over time. Those conclusions were replicated in some of the most important longitudinal studies, such as the *Cambridge Study in Delinquent Development* (e.g., Theobald & Farrington, 2013), the National Youth Survey (King, Massoglia, & MacMillan, 2007), and the Criminal Career and Life Course Study (Bersani, Laub, & Nieuwbeerta, 2009). Moreover, Bersani et al. (2009) showed that the effect of good marriages is a cross-gender and cross-sociohistorical context phenomenon, while Savolainen (2009) found that this effect extended to cohabitating unmarried couples. Finally, in the same vein, while a good and/or a stable marriage or cohabitating relationship promotes the reduction of offending, Theobald and Farrington (2013) found that separation has the opposite effect, increasing the effect of offending. The same dichotomous effect was found for employment: While scientific evidence showed that a stable job is followed by a reduction of offending, becoming unemployed is followed by an increase of recidivism (Farrington, Gallagher, Morley, St. Ledger, & West, 1986; Laub et al., 1998; Ramakers, Van Wilsemm Nieuwbeerta, & Dirkzwager, 2016). Finally, moving from a home or city also appears to be a promotor of desistance from crime, though this has been less widely studied. One proposed explanation suggests that moving to a new social environment enables weak or cut ties with the previous delinquent peers, which reduces the likelihood of recidivism (Kirk, 2012). Informal social control is considered crucial in explaining the effect of these life events on desistance from crime (Farrington, in press; Sampson & Laub, 2003). According to informal social control theory (Farrington, in press; Laub et al., 1998), the establishment of new bonds and ties, legally and socially accepted, such as work or marriage, works as "turning points," gradually reducing offending and promoting a conventional lifestyle.

Despite the tremendous impact of these factors on desistance from crime (e.g., Sampson, Laub, & Wimer, 2006), due to the nature of life events, it is extremely difficult (e.g., promoting stable jobs or moving home) or impossible (e.g., promoting faster aging or good marriages) to transform this scientific knowledge into implications for policies or psychosocial interventions. Despite the impossibility of intervening in natural life events, some adult psychosocial problems associated with criminal behavior can be mitigated. In the last 20 years several studies have shown that criminal behavior is related to a set of adult psychological and social problems, such as drug misuse (Bennett et al., 2008), low education (Lochner & Moretti, 2004), mental health problems (Gendreau, Little, & Goggin, 1996; Yu, Geddes, & Fazel, 2012), and inequality (Nivette, 2011), and some of these problems only emerge during early adulthood (see Schulenberg & Zarrett, 2006). Unfortunately, the effect of adult psychosocial strengths and vulnerabilities in promoting desistance from crime in individuals with a serious history of juvenile delinquency remains underexplored.

CHAPTER 2

PORTUGUESE STUDY ON DELINQUENCY AND SOCIAL MARGINALIZATION: MAJOR TOPICS AND RESEARCH QUESTIONS

The Portuguese Study on Delinquency and Social Marginalization has the main aim to address the role of psychological (e.g., mental health), social (e.g., low income), family (e.g., parental separation; exposure to domestic violence), personal adverse experiences (e.g., sexual abuse), and legal (e.g., juvenile justice involvement) problems on persistence in crime and psychosocial problems in young adults with a history of juvenile delinquency. Having considered the theoretical, empirical, and methodological limitations discussed above, eight research aims were formulated, tested, and presented through the following five parts. Each part corresponding to a published and/or submitted to scientific journals:

Article 1: *Long-term predictors of crime desistance in juvenile delinquents: A systematic review of longitudinal studies*. This theme was written by Basto-Pereira, Começanha, Ribeiro, and Maia (2015) and published in *Aggression and Violent Behavior: A review journal.*

The key research question of the first article is: "What are the predictors found during childhood and adolescence that are related to crime desistance in adulthood in individuals with a history of delinquency?" (Basto-Pereira et al., 2015, p. 333) To address this research question, a systematic review of the literature was conducted. Three independent researchers searched by longitudinal studies with no less than five years of follow-up, and the study was conducted in samples of male or female juvenile offenders, evaluating psychological and social factors predicting desistance in crime during adulthood. This theme is not only just an effort to map the predictors of desistance from crime but also to identify methodological and scientific gaps, with a view to improving future research in this field.

Article 2: *Growing up with adversity: From juvenile justice involvement to criminal persistence and psychosocial problems in young adulthood*. Article 2 was written by Basto-Pereira, Miranda, Ribeiro, and Maia (2016) and published in *Child Abuse & Neglect*.

The purpose of this article was to explore the relationship between childhood adverse experiences on crime and social marginalization. Using a total sample of 315 young adults, we carried out three objectives. First, we explored the relationship between each adverse childhood experience (ACE) and juvenile justice involvement. To accomplish this objective, we used a gender, age, and minority matched control study to compare the prevalence of ACE exposure between young adults with official records of juvenile delinquency

($n = 69$) and a community sample ($n = 69$). In the second objective, the relationship between the exposure to each early adverse experience (before the age of 18) and persistence during early adulthood was tested. The third objective evaluated the exposure to each one of these experiences and psychosocial problems in young adults with a history of juvenile delinquency. The measures of psychosocial problems include current drug misuse, mental health problems, unemployment, perceived quality of life, and school grade achievement. The two last objectives were tested using a sample of 75 young adults with official records of juvenile delinquency. The aim of this theme is to contribute to a better understanding of the role of early adversity beyond abuse and neglect. Political recommendations for CPS and the juvenile justice system, as well as new methodological and theoretical insights, are provided.

Article 3: *Early adversity and adult delinquency: The mediational role of mental health in youth offenders.* This theme was written by Basto-Pereira and Maia (2017a) and submitted for publication.

In article 3, we evaluate whether mental health issues are a mediator between childhood adverse experiences and persistence in crime in young adults with a history of juvenile justice involvement. Mental health problems were evaluated in 75 young adults, and direct and indirect effects of mental health problems were tested between the total score of ACE (early adverse experiences) and current self-reported delinquency (D-CRIM, evaluating current criminal behavior). The third article provides a set of recommendations for mental health policies with young offenders.

Article 4: *Needs and achievements of the juvenile justice system: Insights from two empirical studies with Portuguese young adults.* Article 4 was written by Basto-Pereira, Ribeiro, and Maia (2017) and published (online first) in the *International Journal of Offender Therapy and Comparative Criminology*.

This study has two objectives: (1) to explore the relationship between juvenile justice involvement and; (2) juvenile justice measures on; social, psychological, and criminal behavior characteristics during early adulthood. To accomplish the first objective, we used a sample of 315 young adults, 75 of whom have official records of juvenile delinquency, and we created a gender, age bracket, and race/minority matched control group. Sixty-nine young adults from the community were compared with 69 with past juvenile justice involvement with regard to a set of characteristics including self-serving cognitive distortions, self-reported delinquency, the net of arrested friends, occupation, school grade achievement, mental health problems, and drug misuse. The second objective evaluated the predictive ability of juvenile justice detention (vs. juvenile justice measures served in the community) regarding the same psychological, social, and criminal characteristics, after controlling for the main sociodemographic characteristics. This is one of the first studies globally to explore the effect of juvenile justice involvement and particularly juvenile justice measures beyond criminal indicators, including other important outcomes, on the perpetuation of social marginalization (e.g., drug misuse, mental health problems). This work contributes to exploring the future main needs of youths involved with juvenile justice and particularly under detention measures, which will help to create more effective legal measures, which is scientifically, clinically, and particularly politically relevant.

Article 5: *Persistence in crime in young adults with a history of juvenile delinquency: The role of mental health and psychosocial problems*. Article 5 was written by Basto-Pereira and Maia (2017b) and submitted for publication.

The main goal of this work is to explore the relationship between psychosocial problems and criminal indicators during early adulthood in individuals with past juvenile justice involvement. The psychosocial and mental health problems include psychological distress, perceived quality of life, school grade achievement, occupation, addictive behavior, and housing conditions in the last year. Using correlation and regression models, the relationship between psychosocial and mental health problems in current criminal indicators was tested after controlling for the main sociodemographic variables. The study helps in defining the main areas of interventions in adults with histories of juvenile delinquency, thereby contributing to improving justice services, as well as to promoting desistance from crime and social insertion. Insights regarding scientific, legal, and clinical future directions are provided.

CHAPTER 3

METHODS

3.1. PARTICIPANTS AND PROCEDURES

The data of the Portuguese Study on Delinquency and Social Marginalization include 184 males and 136 females ($N = 315$) aged between 18 and 26 years. This research includes two main subsamples: young adults with official records of juvenile delinquency (ORJC) and young adults from the community. The ORJC sample is composed of young adults tracked in 2014–2015 who had juvenile justice involvement in 2010/2011. These youths were identified through 28 Portuguese Probation Offices of Juvenile Justice Offices where they were serving or had finished noncustodial sentences due to juvenile convictions for crimes committed before the age of 15 (juvenile justice measures can be served until the age of 21) or new convictions in adult courts for crimes committed after the age of 16. Young adult participants (18–26 years of age) who met inclusion criteria were invited to participate by the General Direction of Prison and Probation Service of the Ministry of Justice. Of the 219 participants identified, 55.4% were ineligible to participate due to a large number of reasons, including having failed to attend justice offices three (or more) times, where they would have been formally invited to participate in this research project; being transferred to another justice office; emigration; or even living in a closed therapeutic community. Twenty-one individuals refused to participate in the study, representing 9.6% of the 219 participants initially tracked, or 21.9% of the participants receiving the formal invitation from the probation offices of juvenile justice professionals. According to Galea and Tracy (2007), this represents an appropriate participation rate. Seventy-nine participants had adult convictions among young adults with official records of juvenile delinquency, but only 10.7% had had any criminal records in the last 12 months. The community sample was collected by convenience and snowball methods through workplaces, social welfare, universities and other organizations across the country.

This Portuguese Study on Delinquency and Social Marginalization was authorized by the Ethics Committee of the University of Minho and by the General Direction of Prison and Probation Service of the Ministry of Justice — Portugal. Before the collection of any data, the objectives of this research project, the authorization to consult any official records, and the guarantee of confidentiality were explained to each participant. The respondents filled out the informed consent form and completed the questionnaire in a calm and private room. To achieve an acceptable basis of comparison between groups, matched samples were created (see Nagin, Cullen, & Jonson, 2009). Sixty-nine young adults with past official records of juvenile delinquency had exactly the same characteristics as 69 young adults from the community with regard to sex, age bracket, and race/minority characteristics ($N = 138$). Detailed information about the matched and unmatched socio-demographic characteristics can be seen in Table 3.1.

Table 3.1. Socio-demographic Characteristics of Unmatched and Matched Samples.

Characteristics	Unmatched Samples		Matched Samples	
	ORJC ($n = 75$)	CS ($n = 240$)	ORJC ($n = 69$)	CS ($n = 69$)
	n (%)	n (%)	n (%)	n (%)
Sex				
Male	69 (92.00%)	115 (47.92%)	63 (91.30%)	63 (91.30%)
Female	6 (8.00%)	125 (52.08%)	6 (8.70%)	6 (8.70%)
Age brackets				
18–20	45 (60.00%)	135 (56.25%)	44 (63.77%)	44 (63.77%)
21–23	28 (37.33%)	59 (24.58%)	23 (33.33%)	23 (33.33%)
24–26	2 (2.67%)	46 (19.17%)	2 (2.90%)	2 (2.90%)
Race				
White	50 (66.67%)	230 (95.83%)	49 (71.01%)	63 (91.30%)
Black	23 (30.67%)	7 (2.92%)	18 (26.09%)	3 (4.35%)
Other	2 (2.67%)	3 (1.25%)	2 (2.90%)	3 (4.35%)
Immigrant status				
No	67 (89.33%)	237 (98.75%)	62 (89.86%)	67 (97.10%)
Yes	8 (10.67%)	3 (1.25%)	7 (10.14%)	2 (2.90%)
Parental immigrant status				
No	48 (64.00%)	202 (84.87%)	48 (69.57%)	49 (71.01%)
Father (only)	8 (10.67%)	16 (6.72%)	5 (7.25%)	11 (15.94%)

Table 3.1. (*Continued*)

Characteristics	**Unmatched Samples**		**Matched Samples**	
	ORJC ($n=75$) *n* (%)	**CS ($n=240$)** *n* (%)	**ORJC ($n=69$)** *n* (%)	**CS ($n=69$)** *n* (%)
Mother (only)	2 (2.67%)	10 (4.20%)	1 (1.45%)	4 (5.80%)
Both parents	17 (22.67%)	10 (4.20%)	15 (21.74%)	5 (7.25%)
Ethnicity/race				
Majority	44 (58.67%)	194 (81.51%)	44 (63.77%)	44 (63.77%)
Minority	31 (41.33%)	44 (18.49%)	25 (36.23%)	25 (36.23%)
Residential area				
Rural	15 (20.00%)	84 (35.44%)	15 (21.74%)	22 (32.35%)
Urban	60 (80.00%)	153 (64.56%)	54 (78.26%)	46 (67.65%)
Occupation				
Worker	18 (24.00%)	43 (24.00%)	17 (26.64%)	13 (18.84%)
Student	14 (18.67%)	141 (58.75%)	13 (18.84%)	43 (62.23%)
Student-Worker	1 (1.33%)	30 (12.50%)	1 (1.45%)	8 (11.59%)
Without occupation	42 (56.00%)	26 (10.83%)	38 (55.075%)	5 (7.25%)

Note: ORJC, official records of juvenile criminal offenses.

3.2. MEASURES

A socio-demographic questionnaire and social assessment survey. These questionnaires were used to collect data about sex (male/female), age, race/ethnicity (minority/majority), residential area (rural/urban), occupation (student/worker/student-worker/without occupation), race, immigrant status (yes/no), parental immigrant status (no/father/mother/both parents), school grade achievement, living in a social neighborhood (yes/no), number of persons living in the same house, net of current friends who are or had been arrested in the past, addiction problems regarding drug use in the last year (yes/no) and alcohol abuse in the last year (yes/no).

Serious adverse experiences during childhood and/or adolescence. To evaluate childhood and adolescence adverse experiences, the ACE questionnaire was used (Felitti et al., 1998; Portuguese version: Pinto et al., 2014). This measure evaluates self-reported abuse, neglect, and household dysfunction occurring before the age of 18. The ACE questionnaire evaluates 10 dimensions, namely: emotional neglect, physical neglect, emotional abuse, physical abuse, sexual abuse, parental separation/divorce, witnessing domestic violence, substance abuse in the household, incarceration of a household member, or having lived with a person with mental illness. Parental separation/divorce, substance abuse in the household, incarceration of a household member, or having lived with a person with mental illness were classified as "Yes" or "No," while abuse, neglect, and witnessing domestic violence were classified using a Likert scale ranging from "0 = Never" to "4 = Too often". Each ACE dimension was dichotomized using the original authors' guidelines (see Felitti et al., 1998; Basto-Pereira et al., 2016). The original (Felitti et al., 1998) and the Portuguese version

(Pinto et al., 2014) of this questionnaire showed appropriate psychometric characteristics.

Cognitive distortions related to antisocial behavior. The How I Think (HIT) questionnaire (Barriga, Gibbs, Potter, & Liau, 2001; Portuguese version: Veloso, 2013), used in our research project, is a multidimensional measure evaluating self-serving cognitive distortions related to antisocial behavior. The participants classify their agreement with 54 affirmations using a Likert scale ranging from "strongly disagree" to "strongly agree." This questionnaire evaluates four types of cognitive distortions related to antisocial behavior (assuming the worst, blaming others, self-centered, minimizing/mislabeling) and provides a total score for these dimensions. The original (Barriga et al., 2001) and the Portuguese version (Veloso, 2013) of the HIT questionnaire showed good psychometric properties and satisfactory levels of internal consistency.

Psychopathological symptoms and general mental health state. The total score for the BSI is considered a general indicator of mental health, evaluating psychological distress and psychopathological symptoms (Derogatis, 1993; Portuguese version: Canavarro, 1999). The questionnaire comprises 53 questions, and each participant classifies the frequency ("0 = Never" to "4 = Very often") of each psychological symptom in the last seven days, using a Likert scale. The BSI includes three general dimensions: (1) the global severity index; (2) the positive symptom index; (3) total symptom index; and nine dimensions: (1) somatization; (2) depression; (3) anxiety; (4) interpersonal sensitivity; (5) phobic anxiety; (6) obsessive-compulsivity; (7) hostility; (8) paranoid ideation; and (9) psychoticism. The original (Derogatis, 1993) and the Portuguese version (Canavarro, 1999) of the BSI showed appropriate psychometric proprieties. The BSI dimensions used in the current research project showed excellent psychometric proprieties, both in the community and ORJC samples.

Perceived quality of life. The EUROHIS-QOL-8 (Power, 2003; Portuguese version: Pereira, Melo, Gameiro, & Canavarro, 2011) was used in this research project to evaluate perceived quality of life. The EUROHIS-QOL-8 is a unidimensional questionnaire with eight items. This five-point Likert scale is used to evaluate different dimensions of quality of life and obtain a total score. The original (Power, 2003) and the Portuguese version (Pereira et al., 2011) of the EUROHIS-QOL-8 showed appropriate psychometric characteristics. The perceived quality-of-life dimensions used in this research project showed good internal consistency for both samples.

Self-reported delinquency. To evaluate self-reported delinquency, the Self-Report Questionnaire for Measuring Delinquency and Crime (D-CRIM) was used. This is a short questionnaire (Basto-Pereira, Miranda, Ribeiro, & Maia, in press) and is composed of two dimensions: (a) self-reported delinquency during the lifetime; and (b) in the last 12 months. Each dimension evaluates the presence of 12 criminal behaviors, ranging from low (e.g., theft, vandalism) to medium (e.g., robbery) or even serious criminality (e.g., homicide). Both dimensions evaluate the diversity of criminal behavior during the two different time frames. The D-CRIM measure was developed for the Portuguese population and showed adequate psychometric properties for use with young adults.

Adult convictions. Official records regarding the date and the type of adult criminal convictions were collected at the time of the evaluation through the General Direction of Prison and Probation Service records. All the participants of our sample had at least 24 months of risk for criminal convictions because in Portugal, adult criminal convictions are possible from the age of 16, and all the participants were at least 18 years of age.

3.3. ANALYTIC STRATEGY

SPSS 22.0 and R softwares were used to perform statistical analyses (SPSS; Version 22.0, Chicago, IL, USA). In order to create an acceptable basis to compare both samples (with and without past juvenile justice involvement), a sex, age bracket, and race/minority matched control group was created (n = 138,69 individuals per sample). Statistical analysis was conducted using the χ^2 test, correlations, the t-student test, and regression models, while the mediational model was obtained by calculating the direct and indirect effects of early adverse experiences on current self-reported delinquency using the bootstrapping method. Mathematical assumptions were tested and satisfied for each statistical analysis.

3.4. METHODOLOGIC LIMITATIONS

Regarding article 1, our systematic review has two main limitations (Basto-Pereira et al., 2015). The first limitation is that gray literature has not been included and this might increase the effect of a positive-results publication bias (Dickersin, 1997; Rothstein, Sutton, & Borenstein, 2005). Nonetheless, the majority of the dimensions evaluated in our studies were not significant. It is recommended that future systematic reviews should include a meta-analysis of the findings regarding long-term predictors of desistance from crime, which should include and control for the impact of gray literature. The second limitation was that we considered different ways of evaluating the persistence of criminal activity, which could be another source of bias. Consequently, it is recommended that future meta-analyses should include different outcomes while controlling for the differential impact of each outcome.

With regard to our data collection methods, the major limitation of our study was the absence of a longitudinal prospective design. As suggested by our systematic review (Basto-Pereira et al., 2015), studies following a large number of individuals with criminal careers from childhood to adulthood represent a very small percentage of the studies that have been conducted. Although it is tremendously difficult to implement this type of design, prospective longitudinal studies are very important when attempting to understand juvenile and adult offenders' pathways.

The other major limitation was the sample size. When we compared individuals with and without official records of criminal offenses, our sample included 138 young adults of the same gender, age bracket, and race/minority. In addition, 75 young adults with official records of juvenile delinquency were used in the remaining studies. Future studies should be conducted in larger longitudinal samples, despite the difficulties associated with time, bureaucracy, and funding.

The small number of females in the ORJC sample was also an important limitation. However, the ratio between males and females in the ORJC sample is very close to the ratio of males and females with official records of juvenile delinquency in Portugal in 2011 (Directorate-General of Social Rehabilitation, 2012). This provides an accurate representation of a mixed Portuguese sample of individuals with past official records of juvenile delinquency.

With regard to the measures used in this study, the use of self-reported questionnaires was a major limitation because of the risk of bias, particularly regarding the evaluation of past experiences (see Pinto et al., 2014). However, it is rare for studies to use multimethod research strategies or more accurate measures. Therefore, improving the assessment method is tremendously important because it will increase the accuracy of the current knowledge about delinquency and crime.

Finally, the community sample (*n* = 240) was collected using the convenience sampling method, which was a significant limitation. Nonetheless, the use of a control group that matched the gender, age brackets, and race/minority between samples allowed us to mitigate some of the potential bias associated with this type of sampling, and it enabled us to create an acceptable basis for comparison between the groups (see Nagin et al., 2009; Wang, Blomberg, & Li, 2005).

CHAPTER 4

JUVENILE DELINQUENCY, CRIME AND SOCIAL MARGINALIZATION: MAIN FINDINGS

This work has the main purpose of advancing knowledge about the importance of the different psychological, social, justice, and family factors that influence persistence in crime, and psychosocial problems in young adults with a history of juvenile delinquency. The findings and considerations of this set of studies is divided in four topics: (a) Psychological and social predictors of desistance from crime in individuals with a history of juvenile delinquency; (b) Juvenile justice involvement, criminal persistence, and psychosocial problems during young adulthood: The role of early adverse experiences; (c) Persistence in crime and psychosocial problems: The role of juvenile justice measures; and (d) Persistence in crime in young adults with a record of juvenile delinquency.

4.1. PSYCHOLOGICAL AND SOCIAL PREDICTORS OF DESISTANCE FROM CRIME IN INDIVIDUALS WITH A HISTORY OF JUVENILE DELINQUENCY

In the work entitled *Long-Term Predictors of Crime Desistance in Juvenile Delinquents: A Systematic Review of Longitudinal Studies*, a systematic review of prospective longitudinal studies was conducted (Basto-Pereira et al., 2015). When conducting this review, we only included studies that had five or more years of follow-up with individuals that had a history of juvenile delinquency. This study was the first systematic review that has evaluated the long-term predictors of desistance from crime (Basto-Pereira et al., 2015; Farrington, in press). This study also aimed to evaluate the childhood and adolescent predictors of desistance from crime when the individuals had a history of juvenile delinquency. A total of 23 different dimensions evaluating desistance from crime in more than one study were found (Basto-Pereira et al., 2015). Surprisingly, none of the predictors found in multiple studies were a systematically significant predictor of desistance from crime in adults with a history of juvenile delinquency. While sexual abuse, severe disciplinary practices, family criminal history for females, hyperactivity, extroversion, aggressivity, verbal IQ, general IQ, alcohol abuse, substance abuse, and academic levels for males were inconsistently significant across the studies, the remaining factors (e.g., parental supervision, prosocial behavior, impulsivity) were consistently nonsignificant predictors of desistance from criminal activity (Basto-Pereira et al., 2015).

In fact, a large number of dimensions were systematically nonsignificant predictors of desistance from crime across the studies. One strong hypothesis for this phenomenon is that the major predictors of juvenile delinquency are equally present in the past of individuals with a serious history of juvenile delinquency, regardless of whether or not these individuals continue to engage in criminal activity during adulthood (Basto-Pereira et al., 2015). That is in the line of article 2, since we found four early adverse experiences correlated with juvenile justice involvement, but only one early adverse experience was related with persistence in crime in individuals with history of juvenile delinquency. As Loeber et al. (2007) conclusions, our findings also suggest that desisters from crime and persisters share a large proportion of risk factors that are not present in individuals without a history of juvenile delinquency.

This study has also shown that a significant number of dimensions evaluated as predictors of desistance from crime were inconsistently significant across the studies. One possible explanation for this (apart from the methodological differences across the studies, with regard to when and how each predictor and outcome were assessed) is that repeated criminal activity is not independent from the set of factors that promotes social exclusion in the present. Examples of these factors include current mental illness and addiction problems. Consequently, in article 1 we stated that: "to test predictors of long-term crime desistance, without simultaneously assessing social insertion in the present can lead to different results between studies" (Basto-Pereira et al., 2015, p. 340). In the same line, article 2 (Basto-Pereira et al., 2016), article 3 (Basto-Pereira & Maia, 2017a), and article 4 (Basto-Pereira et al., 2017) showed that early adverse experiences and juvenile justice system involvement are related to indicators of social marginalization during early adulthood (e.g., current misuse of drugs, unemployment, mental health), while article 5 showed that adult mental health problems and misuse of drugs are related to criminal indicators (Basto-Pereira & Maia, 2017b).

4.2. JUVENILE JUSTICE INVOLVEMENT, CRIMINAL PERSISTENCE AND PSYCHOSOCIAL PROBLEMS DURING YOUNG ADULTHOOD: THE ROLE OF EARLY ADVERSE EXPERIENCES

The main purpose of the work entitled *Growing Up with Adversity: From Juvenile Justice Involvement, to Persistence in Crime and Psychosocial Problems* was to deepen the relationship between each type of early adverse experience that occurred before the age of 18, and juvenile justice system involvement, persistence in criminal activity, and psychosocial problems during early adulthood (Basto-Pereira et al., 2016).

The most impressive finding was the fact that, after controlling for gender, age, race, and ethnicity, 7 out of 10 self-reported adverse experiences were significantly more prevalent among individuals with past juvenile justice system involvement, as compared to others in the community (Basto-Pereira et al., 2016). When conducting a multivariate data analysis, four of these experiences (i.e., physical abuse, sexual abuse, parental separation or divorce, and incarceration of household members) were found to be independent predictors of official record of juvenile delinquency. In contrast, only sexual abuse during childhood or adolescence predicted current persistence in crime for those individuals with a past history of juvenile delinquency.

As highlighted by Farrington (in press) and Moffitt (2006), childhood and adolescent risk factors are considerably relevant indicators of adult criminal behavior. In addition, the meta-analysis conducted by Braga et al. (2017) showed that all types of abuse and neglect were predictors of juvenile aggressive antisocial behavior, with sexual abuse being the strongest longitudinal predictor.

Both articles *Growing Up with Adversity: From Juvenile Justice Involvement, to Persistence in Crime and Psychosocial Problems* and *Early adversity and adult delinquency: The mediational role of mental health in youth offenders* (Basto-Pereira et al., 2016; Basto-Pereira & Maia, 2017a) have provided some explanations of the relationship between early adverse experiences and criminal outcomes, particularly when there is continued exposure to stressful situations, such as exposure to domestic violence or physical abuse, the biologic stress system, and the maturation of brain structures can be affected (Lee & Hoaken, 2007; Watts-English, Fortson, Gibler, Hooper, & DeBellis, 2006). Healthy, mature brain structures, particularly with regard to those areas that have evolved to regulate the biological stress system, play a central role in an individual's ability to develop control mechanisms, regulate emotions, and regulate behaviors, which are essential abilities not only for the prevention of antisocial and criminal behavior but also to ensure good mental health (Lee & Hoaken, 2007; Roberton, Daffern, & Bucks, 2012).

While early adverse experiences play an important role in juvenile delinquency, mental health appears to be a key mediating feature and risk factor for future criminal outcomes among individuals with a history of juvenile delinquency. First, in the second article (*Growing Up with Adversity*), psychological distress was the psychosocial problem with the highest number of significant, or marginally significant, predictors among all of the serious adverse experiences (Basto-Pereira et al., 2016). Second, in part 3, the mental health problems indicator partially mediated the link between childhood adverse experiences and current self-reported delinquency in individuals with past juvenile justice involvement (Basto-Pereira & Maia, 2017a). Finally, in the fifth manuscript (*Persistence in crime in young adults with a history of juvenile delinquency: The role of mental health and psychosocial problems*), mental health indicator has the strongest relationship to the criminal indicators that we evaluated (Basto-Pereira & Maia, 2017b). Therefore, all of our research suggests that mental health plays an important role in individuals with a history of juvenile delinquency.

We also found other current psychosocial problems related to early adverse experiences. These problems include low quality-of-life perception and poor grade achievement in school. Of particular interest is the fact that each adverse experience appears to play an independent role in social marginalization. More specifically, while emotional neglect appears to be specifically related to future psychosocial problems, having an incarcerated household member was specifically related to antisocial and criminal outcomes. As far as we know, our research is the first to explore the independent role of each adverse experience during childhood, beyond abuse and neglect, and the relationship with a wide range of psychosocial dysfunctions in individuals with a history of juvenile criminal behavior.

4.3. PERSISTENCE IN CRIME AND PSYCHOSOCIAL PROBLEMS: THE ROLE OF JUVENILE JUSTICE MEASURES

The article 4, entitled *Needs and Achievements of the Juvenile Justice System: Insights From Two Empirical Studies with Portuguese Young Adults*, aimed to identify the future needs of young adults who are a part of the juvenile justice system. This article also attempted to identify the different needs of young adults serving institutionalized sentences, as opposed to young adults serving sentences in the community (Basto-Pereira et al., 2017).

In the first objective, we explored the role of past juvenile justice system involvement on psychological, social, and criminal outcomes during early adulthood. Our findings suggest that individuals with past juvenile justice system involvement have significantly lower levels of school achievement and occupational achievement, and higher levels of arrested friends, misuse of drugs, self-reported delinquency in the last 12 months, and self-serving cognitive distortions related to antisocial behavior when compared with individuals from the community, even after controlling for the variables of gender, age, and race/ethnicity.

Our findings highlight the high number of criminal and psychosocial problems in young individuals with a past history of juvenile justice system involvement. More specifically, with regard to occupation, achievement in school, and the current number of arrested friends, we found that there were large differences between individuals with past juvenile justice system involvement, as opposed to those without past juvenile justice system involvement. These results are very concerning, because, as we stated in the fourth article: *over the long term, school failure, lack of a functional daily occupation and large group of deviant friends provide the perfect conditions for criminal persistence (lack of money, time available and partners in crime)* (Basto-Pereira et al., 2017, p. 14). As we advanced with our research (Basto-Pereira et al., 2017), it became apparent that labeling and deviant peer contamination effects are important mechanisms to explain the relationship between juvenile justice involvement, future criminal behavior, and persistence in criminal activity during young adulthood. In addition, having a more adverse and vulnerable situation increases the risk of juvenile justice involvement and strongly affects the level and quality of formal education, as well as future career opportunities

(Blair & Diamond, 2008; Gatti et al., 2009; Naswall & De Witte, 2003).

The second objective was to evaluate the predictive ability that past detention measures have on criminal, social, and psychological outcomes once an individual becomes a young adult. We found that sentences in "educational centers," as opposed to sentences served in the community, predicted marginally significant higher number of deviant friends (i.e., the number of current friends who are or were arrested) and self-reported delinquency in the last 12 months, even after controlling for age, gender, race/ethnicity, and delinquency during lifetime. With regard to the potential iatrogenic effects caused by detention measures, deviant peer contagion is the most plausible explanation. It is expected that young adults sharing accommodation with other convicted adolescents have a higher number of deviant friends and that the number of deviant friends is maintained over time. It is also expected that adults with higher number of deviant friends have higher levels of criminal behavior (e.g., Basto-Pereira et al., 2017; Fergusson, Vitaro, Wanner, & Brendgen, 2007; Simons, Stewart, Gordon, Conger, & Elder, 2002).

Overall, in line of our project findings and international literature (e.g., Bernburg, Krohn, & Rivera, 2006; Gatti et al., 2009; Monahan, Steinberg, & Cauffman, 2009; Osgood & Briddell, 2006; Osgood, Wilson, O'Malley, Bachman, & Johnston, 1996), results from this article suggests that individuals with juvenile justice involvement have a higher number of psychological, social, and criminal problems during adulthood. In addition, when detention measures are also present, the risk of recidivism appears to be even greater (Basto-Pereira et al., 2017).

In contrast, detention measures positively predicted school grade achievement. The detention measures appear to have a protective effect with regard to schooling. The mandatory schooling and supervision provided in detention centers appears to be a very positive aspect of "educational centers" (see Law no. 323-D/2000). This article, in the same vein of our findings throughout this work, suggests that policies focused on education, supervision, and social integration may attenuate the negative effects that are commonly linked to juvenile justice involvement (including detention measures), such as, a history of adverse or vulnerable life conditions, deviant friends, among other factors (e.g., Chamberlain, Leve, & DeGarmo, 2007; Fergusson et al., 2007; Lambie & Randell, 2013; Osgood & Briddell, 2006). Therefore, investment in education policies, in both detention centers and in sentences served in the community, could be a key strategy to break the cycle of social marginalization and criminal behavior.

4.4. PERSISTENCE IN CRIME IN YOUNG ADULTS WITH A RECORD OF JUVENILE DELINQUENCY: THE ROLE OF ADULT PSYCHOSOCIAL PROBLEMS

In articles 1–4, we evaluated the link between childhood and adolescent psychological, social, familial, and criminal factors, as well as the effect that these factors have on adolescent justice system involvement, the persistence in criminal behavior, and social marginalization as young adults. To close our lifecycle approach, in the final article, entitled *Persistence in Crime in Young Adults with a History of Juvenile Delinquency: The Role of Mental Health and Psychosocial Problems*, we explored the link between adult psychosocial problems and adult criminal indicators in individuals with official records of juvenile delinquency. Adult psychosocial problems include mental health problems, perceived quality of life, school achievement, occupational achievement issues, misuse of drugs, and housing conditions. Adult criminal indicators include self-reported delinquency in the last 12 months and self-serving cognitive distortions. This closing article is particularly important because it provides important insight into the policies that could be effective with adults with a history of criminal activity during adolescence. As far as we know, studies that explore the relationship between psychosocial problems and criminal indicators in adults with an official history of juvenile delinquency are very rare. However, these studies are needed in order to deepen our knowledge of the factors that are linked with a desistance from crime.

In the last article, after controlling other theoretically meaningful variables, current drug misuse and psychological distress (which are indicators of mental health problems) were related with self-serving cognitive distortions; psychological distress was also associated with self-reported delinquency in the last 12 months. In addition, school grade achievement was marginally correlated with self-serving cognitive distortions (Basto-Pereira & Maia, 2017b).

As discussed throughout most of the articles, mental health problems appear to play a central role, not only as a negative outcome of early adverse experiences but also mediating the link between early adverse experiences and persistence in crime in young adults with official records of juvenile delinquency. In article 5, the current mental health state was associated with self-serving cognitive distortions and self-reported delinquency in young adults with an official history of juvenile delinquency (Basto-Pereira & Maia, 2017b). As explained throughout this work, adverse experiences, in general, could cause serious damage to an individual's ability to engage in emotional regulation and self-control processes, which are related to mental health and criminal outcomes during adulthood. Moreover, misuse of drugs is also classified as a mental problem (American Psychiatric Association,

2013), and over the years, scientific evidence has suggested that the current misuse of drugs increases the risk of others mental health problems and criminal behavior (e.g., Bennett et al., 2008; Mills, Teeson, Ross, & Peters, 2006; Moore et al., 2007; Weaver et al., 2003).

The role of education is another key feature throughout our work. In article 4, we found a serious school achievement problem among young adults with past juvenile justice system involvement when compared to a matched control group (Basto-Pereira et al., 2017), and in article 5 we found that the level of school achievement is positively correlated with self-serving cognitive distortions. Therefore, education appear to be a central tool for deflecting crime because it not only provides better job opportunities and better salaries but it also helps to keep young adults away from criminogenic environments.

Our work suggests that mental health and education provide major areas of intervention during adulthood and may help to break the criminal cycle, create better life opportunities, and assist with providing a stable life within the law.

CHAPTER 5

RECOMMENDATION FOR POLICIES, INTERVENTIONS, AND FUTURE DIRECTIONS

5.1. RECOMMENDATION FOR POLICIES AND INTERVENTIONS

Some of the most important contributions that result from this work are the many policy recommendations that are provided throughout all of our studies. This section is divided into three parts: (1) examines the implications for prevention policies, (2) examines the implications for intervention policies, and (3) explores the implications for research policies.

In accordance with previous work (Baglivio & Epps, 2015; Braga et al., 2017; Chartier, Walker, & Naimark, 2010; Fox et al., 2015; Wolf et al., 2015), our study suggests an interrelatedness of ACE in addition to the effect that serious adversity has on the perpetration of future criminal acts. Therefore, CPS are one of the best resources available because they can have an impact on the prevention of future criminal acts. We, therefore, recommend the implementation of evidence-based measures and intervention strategies by

CPS in order to screen and stop different forms of abuse, neglect, and household dysfunction. Similarly, whenever possible, CPS should work with families to identify their needs and improve their psychoeducational skills. Parental education should also be used as part of the first line of defence against the perpetration of criminal acts by young adults. Furthermore, evidence-based national guidelines should be created because they will allow CPS to adopt effective screening tools and strategies to detect and stop early deviant and high-risk behavior.

Other pillars of prevention involve school policies. Our findings are in line with a long list of research studies (e.g., Christle, Jolivette, & Nelsom, 2005; Sutherland, 2011), which suggest that school failure and the propensity to commit criminal acts are linked (Basto-Pereira et al., 2017). Schools should have evidence-based guidelines that establish plans for screening and action in situations involving school failure. In addition, schools should have evidence-based guidelines that assist with identifying dysfunctional and high-risk behaviors. All of our research suggest that the best way to prevent criminal behavior and social marginalization during adulthood is to prevent juvenile delinquency in the first place and to mitigate the many associated risk factors (see Basto-Pereira et al., 2015; Basto-Pereira et al., 2016; Basto-Pereira et al., 2017).

With regard to intervention policies in young offenders, services provided by the juvenile justice system play a privileged role in the prevention of adult crime committed by juvenile delinquents. More specifically, several studies have found that juvenile justice system involvement is one of the best predictors of the persistence of criminal activity as an adult (e.g., Sutherland, 2011; Thornberry & Krohn, 2005). As a result of our research, we have been able to suggest four main areas of intervention that need to be addressed by the juvenile justice system. First, the system should screen and address the academic needs of young offenders, regardless of whether the offender is serving their sentence in detention centers or in the community. School is a protective factor for young offenders (Christle et al., 2005; Sutherland, 2011) because it provides a better chance of finding a well-paid, legal job during adulthood. In addition, school provides a less criminogenic environment during adolescence. Therefore, providing school services could significantly reduce the risk of deviant peer contagion and, consequently, recidivism.

Second, our studies suggest that psychopathological symptoms are related to persistence in criminal activity (see Basto-Pereira & Maia, 2017a, 2017b) among young adults with official histories of juvenile delinquency. Consequently, the system should identify and intervene to address the individual's mental health needs because this is important for promoting a stable lifestyle and social integration.

Third, our study suggests that young adults with official records of juvenile delinquency are more likely to have been victims of serious abuse, neglect, or household dysfunction during childhood or adolescence and these adults may have been the victims of more than one of these situations (Basto-Pereira et al., 2016). Consequently, we recommend that the juvenile justice system creates national, evidence-based guidelines to effectively screen and stop serious situations of abuse, neglect, and household dysfunction among young offenders.

Finally, our research indicates (see Basto-Pereira et al., 2017) that cognitive distortions related to antisocial behavior are a distinctive feature among young adults with official records of juvenile delinquency. Therefore, it is recommended that the juvenile justice system should create programs to evaluate and address the cognitive distortions that perpetuate and validate criminal behaviors.

Research policies play a key role in ensuring the effectiveness of all of the recommendations provided. Therefore, we recommend the establishment of protocols between governments and research centers in order to: (1) create evidence-based guidelines for child protective services, juvenile justice services, and schools; (2) create and implement scientific-based juvenile justice measures; (3) help to improve the tools and strategies used to evaluate the needs of young adults and their families; and (4) provide training to teachers, juvenile justice system professionals, and child protection services professionals. Furthermore, these protocols between governments and research centers can be used to create conditions that are conducive to conducting longitudinal research projects that follow the young adults and their families over time, which will allow us to deepen our knowledge of desistance from crime and social integration.

If some of these policies are implemented in the future, then we believe that there will be a significant reduction in the number of juvenile offenses and adult recidivism. We are, however, aware of the significant monetary burden associated with implementing all of these policies, particularly with regard to labor and training costs. Nonetheless, if we consider that the cost of only one chronic offender had been estimated to be between $793,000 and $861,000 (Welsh et al., 2008), and that intervention efforts with young offenders actually work (see Lipsey, 2009), then the benefits far outweigh the costs.

5.2. FUTURE DIRECTIONS

This last section summarizes the most important directive measure that result from the limitations imposed by the literature. It also provides insight into the scientific findings that have been made throughout our research project.

The meta-analysis of studies about desistance from crime is one of the most important steps to establish high-quality intervention techniques, which could help juvenile delinquents. Nonetheless, the quality of the meta-analysis is the result of the general quality of the studies included. Consequently, future research should work on the definition and application of gold-standard measures to evaluate predictors and outcomes (Basto-Pereira et al., 2015). In addition, future research should monitor not only the temporal predictors of persistence in criminal activity but also the psychosocial dimensions during adulthood, such as employment, which probably work as protective factors (Basto-Pereira et al., 2015).

It is also recommended that future research should work on improving the current measures that are used to evaluate abuse, neglect, and other types of adversity. As we suggested in article 2 (Basto-Pereira et al., 2016), additional questions should be addressed when early adverse experiences are evaluated; more specifically, questions as: "When did it happen?," "Who is responsible?," and "What was the perceived response?" Otherwise, the same dimensions could be evaluated as equal in very different situations because, as we argued in article 2: *the long-term effect of physical abuse resulting from a street fight between gangs during adolescence (with the perceived resources to protect themselves) could be very different from the effects caused by frequent parental beating[s] during childhood* (Basto-Pereira et al., 2016, p. 73).

In article 2, we found additional interesting and unexplored ideas that provide future directions; for example, the only predictor of persistence in crime among individuals with official records of juvenile delinquency was sexual abuse

(Basto-Pereira et al., 2016). This result is in line with the meta-analysis of longitudinal studies conducted by Braga et al. (2017), which shows that child sexual abuse is the strongest predictor of aggressive antisocial behaviors among juveniles. Because the effect of size was much greater than in previous longitudinal studies (O.R. > 4.5), we dug deeper into this question. We found that the mean age for the first sexual abuse was 15.6 years of age. It should be noted that one of the criteria on the ACE questionnaire for sexual abuse is that the sexual intercourse occurs before the individual turns 18 and with a person aged five years or older. Because our study is, to some extent, retrospective, and previous studies have shown that delinquency is related to having older friends, and having older friends is related with early sexual initiation (e.g., Collins et al., 2004; McAdams, Salekin, Marti, Lester, & Barker, 2014), we advanced the following question, *Is it possible that juvenile delinquency is a risk factor for sexual abuse?* (Basto-Pereira et al., 2016, p. 9). Future studies should test this hypothesis.

In article 3, we presented one of the first studies that has tested the role of mental health on the relationship between early adversity and adult crime. Our findings suggest that mental health problems partially mediate the relationship between early adverse experiences and current self-reported delinquency. Similarly, article 5 indicates that mental health is related to current self-serving cognitive distortions and self-reported delinquency. Future studies should explore the importance of the role that mental health has on recidivism among youth offenders. In addition, future studies should also explore the role of other factors mediating the link between serious adversity at a young age and criminal behavior.

Finally, during our research (Basto-Pereira et al., 2017) we explored the role of juvenile justice system involvement and the differential role of past detention measures, as opposed to measures served in the community. It is recommended that future studies should look deeper into this topic, by using larger samples and providing more accurate research designs. In addition, future studies should review the role that is played by each type of measure served in the community, not only with regard to criminal outcomes but also in relation to social integration.

CHAPTER 6

OVERALL CONCLUSIONS

One of the strengths of this study was that it went beyond criminal outcomes by exploring the role of other important dimensions during adulthood, such as mental health problems, misuse of drugs, and perceived quality of life outcomes. Consequently, our work provides many insights into the role that family, psychosocial, and legal factors play during adolescence and early adulthood, and how they relate to the trajectories associated with desistance from crime and social integration as a young adult.

The findings from the first three objectives suggest that the majority of risk factors for juvenile delinquency remain present among adults with official records of juvenile delinquency, whether or not they desist from criminal activity (Basto-Pereira et al., 2015, 2016). Therefore, we suggest that the best way to promote desistance from criminal activity is to prevent juvenile delinquency in the first place. The second, third, and fourth studies (Basto-Pereira et al., 2016) have suggested that early adverse experiences appear to play a major role in promoting involvement in the justice system and psychosocial problems. We have provided a set of recommendations for CPS and juvenile justice services, which will help prevent, screen, and stop serious cases of adversity. The findings from article five (Basto-Pereira & Maia, 2017a) indicate that mental health problems are one of the links that explains the relationship between early adversity and adult criminal activity. In addition, adult mental health problems appear to be related to criminal thinking and behavior during adulthood for individuals that have an official history of juvenile delinquency (Basto-Pereira & Maia, 2017b). Therefore, we suggest the development of a set of mental health policies for individuals with past involvement in the juvenile justice system.

Finally, the findings from the sixth and seventh objectives (Basto-Pereira et al., 2017) suggest that psychosocial, criminal, academic, and social problems are linked with juvenile justice system involvement, while juvenile detention and institutionalization measures appear to be related to considerably worse criminal outcomes. We have, therefore, provided a large set of recommendations to prevent iatrogenic effects, such as recidivism, to promote desistance from criminal activity, and to promote social integration.

REFERENCES

Alves, J., Dutra, A., & Maia, Â. (2013). História de adversidade, saúde e psicopatologia em reclusos: Comparação entre homens e mulheres [History of adversity, health and psychopathology among prisoners: Comparison between men and women]. *Ciência & Saúde Coletiva*, *18*(3), 701–709. doi:10.1590/S1413-81232013000300016

Alves, J., & Maia, Â. (2010). Experiências adversas durante a infância e comportamentos de risco para a saúde em mulheres reclusas [Adverse childhood experiences and health risk behaviours in female prisoners]. *Psicologia, Saúde & Doenças*, *11*(1), 151–171.

American Psychiatric Association. (2013). *Diagnostic and statistical manual of mental disorders* (5th ed.). Washington, DC: APA.

Baglivio, M. T., & Epps, N. (2015). The interrelatedness of adverse childhood experiences among high-risk juvenile offenders. *Youth Violence and Juvenile Justice*, *14*(3), 1 20. doi:10.1177/1541204014566286

Barriga, A. Q., Gibbs, J. C., Potter, G., & Liau, A. K. (2001). *The how i think questionnaire manual*. Champaign, IL: Research Press.

Basto-Pereira, M., Começanha, R., Ribeiro, S., & Maia, A. (2015). Long-term predictors of crime desistance in juvenile delinquents: A systematic review of longitudinal studies. *Aggression and Violent Behavior, A Review Journal*, *25*(B), 332–342. doi:10.1016/j.avb.2015.09.012

Basto-Pereira, M., & Maia, A. (2017a). *Early adversity and adult delinquency: The mediational role of mental health in youth offenders*. Manuscript submitted.

Basto-Pereira, M., & Maia, A. (2017b). *Persistence in crime in young adults with a history of juvenile delinquency: The role of mental health and psychosocial problems*. Manuscript submitted.

Basto-Pereira, M., Miranda, A., Ribeiro, S., & Maia (2016). Growing up with adversity: From juvenile justice involvement, to criminal persistence and psychosocial problems in young adulthood. *Child Abuse and Neglect*, *62*, 63–75. doi:10.1016/j.chiabu.2016.10.011

Basto-Pereira, M., Miranda, A., Ribeiro, S., & Maia, Â. (in press). The psychometric properties of a questionnaire for measuring delinquency and crime (D-CRIM). In n/a (Ed.), *Avances en Psicología Clínica, 2015*. Granada, Espanã: Asociación Española de Psicología Conductual.

Basto-Pereira, M., Ribeiro, S., & Maia, A. (2017). Needs and achievements of the juvenile justice system: Insights from two empirical studies with Portuguese young adults. *International Journal of Offender Therapy and Comparative Criminology*. Advance online publication. doi:10.1177/0306624X17690450.

Bennett, T., Holloway, K., & Farrington, D. (2008). The effectiveness of neighborhood watch. *Campbell*

Collaboration systematic review final report. Retrieved from http://campbellcollaboration.org/lib/download/248/

Bernburg, J. G., & Krohn, M. D. (2003). Labeling, life chances, and adult crime: The direct and indirect effects of official intervention in adolescence on crime in early adulthood. *Criminology*, *41*, 1287–1319.

Bersani, B., Laub, J., & Nieuwbeerta, P. (2009). Marriage and desistance from crime in the Netherlands: Do gender and socio-historical context matter? *Journal of Quantitative Criminology*, *25*, 3–24.

Björkenstam, E., Dalman, C., Vinnerljung, B., Weitoft, G. R., Walder, D. J., & Burstrom, B. (2016). Childhood household dysfunction, school performance and psychiatric care utilization in young adults: A register study of 96 399 individuals in Stockholm County. *Journal of Epidemiology and Community Health*, *70*(5), 473–480. doi:10.1111/add.13454.

Blair, C., & Diamond, A. (2008). Biological processes in prevention and intervention: The promotion of self-regulation as a means of preventing school failure. *Development and Psychopathology*, *20*, 899–911.

Blonigen, D. M. (2010). Explaining the relationship between age and crime: Contributions from the developmental literature on personality. *Clinical Psychology Review*, *30*, 89–100. doi:10.1016/j.cpr.2009.10.001

Bouchery, E. E., Harwood, H. J., Sacks, J. J., Simon, C. J., & Brewer, R. D. (2011). Economic costs of excessive alcohol consumption in the U.S. 2006. *American Journal of Preventive Medicine*, *41*(5), 516–524.

Braga, T., Gonçalves, L. C., Basto-Pereira, M., & Maia, A. (2017). Unraveling the link between maltreatment and juvenile antisocial behavior: A meta-analysis of prospective longitudinal studies. *Aggression and Violent Behavior*, *33*, 37–50. doi:10.1016/j.avb.2017.01.006.

Canavarro, C. (1999). Inventário de sintomas psicopatológicos—BSI [Brief Symptom Inventory—BSI]. In M. R. Simões & M. M. Gonçalves (Eds.), *Testes e provas psicológicas em Portugal* (pp. 95–109). Braga: Associação dos Psicólogos Portugueses/Sistemas Humanos e Organizacionais.

Caspi, A., & Roberts, W. B. (2010). Personality development across the life course: The argument for change and continuity. *Psychological Inquiry*, *12*(2), 49–66. doi:10.1207/S15327965PLI1202_01

Chamberlain, P., Leve, L. D., & DeGarmo, D. S. (2007). Multidimensional treatment foster care for girls in the juvenile justice system: 2-year follow-up of a randomized clinical trial. *Journal of Consulting and Clinical Psychology*, *75*(1), 187–193. doi:10.1037/0022-006X.75.1.187

Chartier, M. J., Walker, J. R., & Naimark, B. (2010). Separate and cumulative effects of adverse childhood experiences inpredicting adult health and health care utilization. *Child Abuse & Neglect*, *34*(6), 454–464. doi:10.1016/j.chiabu.2009.09.020

Christle, C. A., Jolivette, K., & Michael Nelson, C. (2005). Breaking the school to prison pipeline: Identifying school risk and protective factors for youth delinquency. *Exceptionality: A Special Education Journal*, *13*(2), 69–88. doi:10.1207/s15327035ex1302_2

Cohen, M. (1998). The monetary value of saving a high risk youth. *Journal of Quantitative Criminology*, *14*, 5–34.

Collins, R. L., Elliott, M. N., Berry, S. H., Kanouse, D. E., Kunkel, D., Hunter, S. B., & Miu, A. (2004). Watching sex on television predicts adolescent initiation of sexual behavior. *Pediatrics*, *114*, 280–289. doi:10.1542/peds.2003-1065-L

Day, D. M., Bevc, I., Theodor, F., Rosenthal, J. S., & Duchesne, T. (2008). Change and continuity in criminal offending: Criminal trajectories of the "Toronto" sample. *Final report submitted to the Ministry of Children and Youth Services*, Toronto, Ontario. Retrieved from https://tinyurl.com/jlznu7y

Derogatis, L. R. (1993). *BSI brief symptom inventory: Administration, scoring, and procedure manual* (4th ed.). Minneapolis, MN: National Computers Systems.

Dickersin, K. (1997). How important is publication bias? A synthesis of available data. *AIDS Education and Prevention*, 9(A), 15–21.

Directorate-General of Social Rehabilitation – Ministry of Justice – DGRSP (2016). *Relatório Estatístico Anual – DGRS 2015 [Annual Statistics Report – DGRSP 2015]*. Lisboa: Direção de Serviços de Estudos e Planeamento. Retrieved from http://tinyurl.com/nmesstb

Directorate-General of Social Rehabilitation (DGRS). (2012). *Auto-avaliac¸ão e relatório de Atividades—DGRS 2011 [Self-assessment and activity Report—DGSR—2011]*. Lisboa: DGRSP. Retrieved from http://tinyurl.com/hv7mdzv

Dodge, K. A., Dishion, T. J., & Lansford, J. E. (2006). *Deviant peer influences in programs for youth (problems and solutions)*. New York, NY: The Guilford Press.

Driessen, M., Schroeder, T., Widmann, B., von Schonfeld, C. E., & Schneider, F. (2006). Childhood trauma, psychiatric disorders, and criminal behavior in prisoners in Germany: A comparative study in incarcerated women and men. *The Journal of Clinical Psychiatry*, 67(10), 1486–1492.

Dube, S. R., Felitti, V. J., Dong, M., Chapman, D. P., Giles, W. H., & Anda, R. F. (2003). Childhood abuse, neglect and household dysfunction and the risk of illicit drug use: The Adverse Childhood Experience Study. *Pediatrics*, *111*, 564–572.

Farrington, D. P. (2003). Key results from the first 40 years of the Cambridge Study in delinquent development. In T. P. Thornberry & M. D. Krohn (Eds.), *Taking stock of delinquency: An overview of findings from contemporary longitudinal studies* (pp. 137–183). New York, NY: Kluwer/ Plenum.

Farrington, D. P. (in press). Childhood risk and protective factors for early desisters, late desisters, and life-course persistent offenders. In n/a (Ed.), *Desistance processes, identity and social bond*. Lisboa: Direção-Geral de Reinserção Social e Serviços Prisionais.

Farrington, D. P., Gallagher, B., Morley, L., St Ledger, R. J., & West, D. J. (1986). Unemployment, school leaving and crime. *British Journal of Criminology*, *26*, 335–356.

Farrington, D. P., Ttofi, M. M., & Coid, J. W. (2009). Development of adolescence limited, late-onset and persistent offenders from age 8 to age 48. *Aggressive Behavior*, *35*, 150–163.

Felitti, V., Anda, R., Nordenberg, D., Williamson, D., Spitz, A., Edwards, V., ... Marks, J. (1998). Relationship of childhood abuse and household dysfunction to many of the leading causes of death in adults. *American Journal of Preventive Medicine, 14*, 245–258.

Fergusson, D. M., Vitaro, F., Wanner, B., & Brendgen, M. (2007). Protective and compensatory factors mitigating the influence of deviant friends on delinquent behaviours during early adolescence. *Journal of Adolescence, 30*, 33–50. doi:10.1016/j.adolescence.2005.05.007

Figueiredo, B., Bifulco, A., Paiva, C., Maia, A., Fernandes, E., & Matos, R. (2004). History of childhood abuse in Portuguese parents. *Child Abuse & Neglect, 28*, 669–682.

Fox, B. H., Perez, N., Cass, E., Baglivio, M. T., & Epps, N. (2015). Trauma changes everything: Examining the relationship between adverse childhood experiences and serious, violent and chronic juvenile offenders. *Child Abuse & Neglect, 46*, 163–173. doi:10.1016/j.chiabu.2015.01.011

Galea, S., & Tracey, M. (2007). Participation rates in epidemiologic studies. *Annals of Epidemiology, 17*, 643–653.

Gatti, U., Tremblay, R. E., & Vitaro, F. (2009). Iatrogenic effect of juvenile justice. *Journal of Child Psychology & Psychiatry, 50*, 991–998. doi:10.1111/j.1469-7610.2008.02057.x

Gendreau, P., Little, T., & Goggin, C. (1996). A meta-analysis of the predictors of adult offender recidivism: What works! *Criminology, 34*, 575–607.

Hawkins, J. D., Herrenkohl, T. I., Farrington, D. P., Brewer, D., Catalano, R. F., Harachi, T. W., & Cothern, L. (2000). *Predictors of youth violence.* Washington, DC: Office of Juvenile Justice and Delinquency Prevention.

Huizinga, D., Schumann, K., Ehret, B., & Elliot, A. (2003). The effects of juvenile justice processing on subsequent delinquent and criminal behavior: A cross-national study. Retrieved from https://www.ncjrs.gov/pdffiles1/nij/grants/205001.pdf

Junger-Tas, J., & Dünkel, F. (2009). *Reforming juvenile justice*. New York, NY: Springer.

Kazemian, L. (2007). Desistance from crime: Theoretical, empirical, methodological, and policy considerations. *Journal of Contemporary Criminal Justice*, *23*(1), 5–27.

Kessler, R. C., McLaughlin, K. A., Green, J. G., Gruber, M. J., Sampson, N. A., Zaslavsky, A. M., ... Williams, D. R. (2010). Childhood adversities and adult psychopathology in the WHO World Mental Health Surveys. *British Journal of Psychiatry*, *197*, 378–385. doi:10.1192/bjp.bp.110.080499

King, R., Massoglia, M., & Macmillan, R. (2007). The context of marriage and crime: Gender, the propensity to marry, and offending in early adulthood. *Criminology*, *45*, 33–65.

Kirk, D. S. (2012). Residential change as a turning point in the life course of crime: Desistance or temporary cessation? *Criminology*, *50*, 329–357. doi:10.1111/j.1745-9125.2011.00262.x

Lambie, I., & Randell, I. (2013). The impact of incarceration on juvenile offenders. *Clinical Psychology Review*, *33*, 448–459. doi:10.1016/j.cpr.2013.01.007

Laub, J. H., Nagin, D. S., & Sampson, R. J. (1998). Trajectories of change in criminal offending: Good marriages and the desistance process. *American Sociological Review*, *63*, 225–238.

Laub, J. H., & Sampson, R. J. (2001). Understanding desistance from crime. *Journal of Crime and Justice*, *28*, 1–70.

Law no. 166/1999 of 14th September 1999: Establishes the Portuguese Guardianship Law.

Law no. 323-D/2000 of 20th December 2000: Establishes the General Regulation for Educational Centers.

Law no. 4/2015 of 15th January 2015: First Amendment to the Portuguese Guardianship Law.

Lee, V., & Hoaken, P. (2007). Cognition, emotion, and neurobiological development: Mediating the relation between maltreatment and aggression. *Child Maltreatment*, *12*, 281–298. doi:10.1177/1077559507303778

Lipsey, M. W. (2009). The primary factors that characterize effective interventions with juvenile offenders: A meta-analytic overview. *Victims and Offenders*, *4*(1), 24–147. doi:10.1080/15564880802612573

Lochner, L., & Moretti, E. (2004). The effect of education on crime: Evidence from prison inmates, arrests, and self-reports. *American Economic Review*, *94*(1), 155–189.

Loeber, R., Pardini, D. A., Stouthamer-Loeber, M., & Raine, A. (2007). Do cognitive, physiological, and psychosocial risk and promotive factors predict desistance from delinquency in males? *Development and Psychopathology*, *19*, 867–887.

Loeber, R., Stouthamer-Loeber, M., Van Kammen, W. B., & Farrington, D. P. (1991). Initiation, escalation, and desistance in juvenile offending and their correlates. *Journal of Criminal Law and Criminology*, *82*, 36–82.

Machado, C., Gonçalves, M., Matos, M., & Dias, A. (2007). Child and partner abuse: Self-reported prevalence and attitudes in the north of Portugal. *Child Abuse & Neglect*, *31*(6), 657–670. doi:10.1016/j.chiabu.2006.11.002

Matsuura, N., Hashimoto, T., & Toichic, M. (2013). Associations among childhood experiences, aggression, depression, and self-esteem in serious female juvenile offenders in Japan. *The Journal of Forensic Psychiatry and Psychology*, *24*(1), 111–127. doi:10.1080/14789949.2012.746384

McAdams, T. A., Salekin, R. T., Marti, C. N., Lester, W. S., & Barker, E. D. (2014). Co-occurrence of antisocial behavior and substance use: Testing for sex differences in the impact of older male friends, low parental knowledge and friends' delinquency. *Journal of Adolescence*, *37*(3), 247–256. doi:10.1016/j.adolescence.2014.01.001

McCollister, K. E., French, M. T., & Fang, H. (2010). The cost of crime to society: New crime-specific estimates for policy and program evaluation. *Drug Alcohol Dependence*, *108*(1–2), 98–109.

Mesquita, C., Basto-Pereira, M., & Maia, A. (2017). Prevalence of childhood victimization experiences in psychiatric patients: A systematic review. *International Journal of Mental Health and Addiction*, *15*(4), 967–984. doi:10.1007/s11469-016-9697-8

Mills, K. L., Teeson, M., Ross, J., & Peters, L. (2006). Trauma, PTSD, and substance use disorders: Findings from the Australian National Survey of Mental Health and WellBeing. *American Journal of Psychiatry*, *163*, 652–658.

Moeller, T. (2001). *Youth aggression and violence: A psychological approach*. Mahwah: Erlbaum.

Moffitt, T. E. (1993). Adolescence-limited and life-course-persistent antisocial behaviour: A developmental taxonomy. *Psychological Review*, *100*(4), 674–701.

Moffitt, T. E. (2006). A review of research on the taxonomy of lifecourse-persistent versus adolescence-limited antisocial behavior. In F. T. Cullen, J. P. Wright, & K. R. Blevins (Eds.), *Taking stock: The status of criminological theory* (pp. 277–311). New Brunswick, NJ: Transaction.

Moffitt, T. E., & Caspi, A. (2001). Childhood predictors differentiate life-course persistent and adolescence-limited antisocial pathways among males and females. *Development and Psychopathology*, *13*, 355–375.

Moffitt, T. E., Caspi, A., Harrington, H., & Milne, B. J. (2002). Males on the life-course-persistent and adolescence-limited antisocial pathways: Follow-up at age 26 years. *Development and Psychopathology*, *14*, 179–207.

Monahan, K. C., Steinberg, L., & Cauffman, E. (2009). Affiliation with antisocial peers, susceptibility to peer influence, and antisocial behavior during the transition to adulthood. *Developmental Psychology*, *45*(6), 1520–1530.

Moore, T. H. M., Zammit, S., Lingford-Hughes, A., Barnes, T. R. E., Jones, P. B., Burke, M., & Lewis, G. (2007). Cannabis use and risk of psychotic or affective mental health outcomes: A systematic review. *The Lancet*, *370*, 319–328. doi:10.1016/S0140-6736(07)61162-3

Nagin, D. S., Cullen, F. T., & Jonson, C. L. (2009). Imprisonment and reoffending. In Michael Tonry (Ed.), *Crime and justice: A review of research* (pp. 115–200). Chicago, IL: University of Chicago Press.

Naswall, K., & De Witte, H. (2003). Who feels insecure in Europe? Predicting job insecurity from background variables. *Economic and Industrial Democracy*, *24*(2), 189–215. doi:10.1177/0143831X03024002003

National Institute of Statistics – Portugal. (2016). *Resident population by sex and age – 2015*. Retrieved from https://www.ine.pt/xportal/xmain?xpid=INE&xpgid=ine_indicadores&indOcorrCod=0001223&contexto=bd&selTab=tab2

Nivette, A. (2011). Cross-national predictors of crime: A meta-analysis. *Homicide Studies*, *15*(2), 103–131. doi:10.1177/1088767911406397

Osgood, D. W., & O'Neill Briddell, L. (2006). Peer effects in juvenile justice. In K. Dodge, T. Dishion, & J. Lansford (Eds.), *Deviant peer influences in programs for youth: Problems and solutions* (pp. 141–161). New York, NY: Guilford Press.

Osgood, W., Wilson, J. K., O'Malley, P. M., Bachman, J. G., & Johnston, L. D. (1996). Routine activities and individual deviant behavior. *American Sociological Review*, *61*(4), 635–655.

Pereira, M., Melo, C., Gameiro, S., & Canavarro, M. C. (2011). Estudos psicométricos da versão em Português Europeu do índice de qualidade de vida EUROHIS-QOL-8 [Psychometric studies of the Portuguese version of the quality of life index EUROHIS-QOL-8]. *Laboratório de Psicologia*, *9*, 109–123. doi:10.14417/lp.627

Pinto, R., Correia, L., & Maia, Â. C. (2014). Assessing the reliability of retrospective reports of adverse childhood experiences among adolescents with documented childhood maltreatment. *Journal of Family Violence*, *29*, 431–438. doi:10.1007/s10896-014-9602-9

Pinto, R. J., & Maia, Â. C. (2013). Psychopathology, physical complaints and health risk behaviors among youth who were victims of childhood maltreatment: A comparison between home and institutional interventions. *Children and Youth Services Review*, *35*(4), 603–610. doi:10.1016/j.childyouth.2013.01.008

Power, M. (2003). Development of a common instrument for quality of life. In A. Nosikov & C. Gudex (Eds.), *EUROHIS: Developing common instruments for health surveys* (pp. 145–159). Amsterdam: IOS Press.

Ramakers, A. A. T., Van Wilsem, J., Nieuwbeerta, P., & Dirkzwager, A. (2016). Returning to a former employer: A potentially successful pathway to ex-prisoner re-employment. *British Journal of Criminology*, *56*(4), 668–688. doi:10.1093/bjc/azv063

Regoli, R. M., Hewitt, J. D., & DeLisi, M. (2011). *Delinquency in society: The essentials.* Boston, MA: Jones & Bartlett.

Ribeiro, S. (2015). *Comportamento delinquente em jovens com vitimação autorreportada e em registo oficial [Delinquent behavior in youths with self-report and official records of victimization].* Tese de mestrado/Master's thesis. Escola de Psicologia da Universidade do Minho, Braga, Portugal. Retrieved from https://repositorium.sdum.uminho.pt/bitstream/1822/37606/1/Disserta%C3%A7%C3%A3o%20Sofia%20Ribeiro.pdf

Ribeiro, S., Basto-Pereira, M., & Maia, A. (2016). Intergenerational impact of mental illness in juveniles with history of victimization. *Psicologia, Saúde & Doenças*, *17*(1), 74–81. doi:10.15309/16psd170111

Rijo, D., Brazão, N., Barroso, R., Ribeiro da Silva, D., Vagos, P., Vieira, A., ... Macedo, A. M. (2016). Mental health problems in male young offenders in custodial versus community based-programs: Implications for juvenile justice interventions. *Child and Adolescent Psychiatry and Mental Health*, *10*(40), 2–12. doi:10.1186/s13034-016-0131-6

Roberton, T., Daffern, M., & Bucks, R. S. (2012). Emotion regulation and aggression. *Aggression and Violent Behavior: A Review Journal*, *17*(1), 72–82. doi:10.1016/j.avb.2011.09.006

Roberts, A., Yang, M., Zhang, T., & Coid, J. (2008). Personality disorder, temperament, and childhood adversity: Findings from a cohort of prisoners in England & Wales. *Journal of Forensic Psychology and Psychiatry*, *19*(4), 460–483.

Rothstein, H. R., Sutton, A. J., & Borenstein, M. (2005). *Publication bias in meta-analysis Prevention, assessment and adjustments*. Hoboken, NJ: Wiley.

Sampson, R. J., & Laub, J. H. (1993). *Crime in the making: Pathways and turning points through life*. Cambridge, MA: Harvard University Press.

Sampson, R. J., & Laub, J. H. (2003). Life-course desisters? Trajectories of crime among delinquent boys followed to age 70. *Criminology*, *41*, 301–339.

Sampson, R., & Laub, J. (2005). When prediction fails: From crime-prone boys to heterogeneity in adulthood. *The Annals of the American Academy of Political and Social Science*, *602*, 73–79.

Sampson, R. J., Laub, J. H., & Wimer, C. (2006). Does marriage reduce crime? A counterfactual approach to within individual causal effects. *Criminology*, *44*, 465–508.

Savolainen, J. (2009). Work, family and criminal desistance: Adult social bonds in a Nordic welfare state. *British Journal of Criminology*, *49*, 285–304.

Schulenberg, J. E., & Zarrett, N. R. (2006). Mental health during emerging adulthood: Continuity and discontinuity in courses, causes, and functions. In J. J. Arnett & J. L. Tanner (Eds.), *Emerging adults in America: Coming of age in the 21st century* (pp. 135–172). Washington, DC: American Psychological Association.

Schwalbe, C. S., Gearing, R. E., MacKenzie, M. J., Brewer, K. B., & Ibrahim, R. (2012). A meta-analysis of experimental studies of diversion programs for juvenile offenders. *Clinical Psychology Review*, *32*, 26–33. doi:10.1016/j.cpr.2011.10.002

Shufelt, J., & Cocozza, J. (2006). Youth with mental health disorders in the juvenile justice system: Results from a multi-state prevalence study. Retrieved from National Center for Mental Health and Juvenile Justice website http://www.ncmhjj.com/pdfs/publications/PrevalenceRPB.pd

Simons, R., Stewart, E., Gordon, L., Conger, R., & Elder, G. H. (2002). A test of life-course explanations for stability and change in antisocial behavior from adolescence to young adulthood. *Criminology*, *40*(2), 401 -434.

Stouthamer-Loeber, M., Wei, E., Loeber, R., & Masten, A. S. (2004). Desistance from persistent serious delinquency in the transition to adulthood. *Development and Psychopathology*, *16*, 897–918.

Sutherland, A. (2011). The relationship between school and youth offending. *Social Policy Journal of New Zealand*, *37*, 1–19.

Sweeten, G. (2006). Who will graduate? Disruption of high school education by arrest and court involvement. *Justice Quarterly*, *23*, 462–480.

Tanner, J., Davies, S., & O'Grady, B. (1999). Whatever happened to yesterday's rebels? Longitudinal effects of youth delinquency on education and employment. *Social Problems*, *46*, 250–274.

Theobald, D., & Farrington, D. P. (2013). The effects of marital breakdown on offending: Results from a prospective longitudinal survey of males. *Psychology, Crime and Law*, *19*, 391–408.

Thornberry, T. P., & Krohn, M. D. (2005). Applying interactional theory to the explanation of continuity and change in antisocial behavior. In D. P. Farrington (Ed.), *Integrated Developmental & Life-course Theories of Offending* (pp. 183–209). London: Transaction Publishers.

United Nations Office on Drugs and Crime. (2017). *UNODC statistics*. Retrieved from https://data.unodc.org

Van der Put, C., Lanctôt, N., Ruiter, C., & Van Vugt, E. (2015). Child maltreatment among boy and girl probationers: Does type of maltreatment make a difference in offending behavior and psychosocial problems? *Child Abuse & Neglect*, *46*, 142–151. doi:10.1016/j.chiabu.2015.05.012

Veloso, A. C. C. (2013). *Validação do How I Think: Questionnaire para a população adulta portuguesa [Portuguese validation of How I Think: Questionnaire for the Portuguese adult population]*. Tese de mestrado não publicada/Unpublished master's thesis. Instituto Superior de Ciências da Saúde Egas Moniz, Lisboa, Portugal.

Verbruggen, J., Blokland, A. A. J., & Van der Geest, V. R. (2012). Effects of employment and unemployment on serious offending in a high-risk sample of men and women from ages 18 to 32 in the Netherlands. *British Journal of Criminology*, 52, 845–869.

Wang, X., Blomberg, T. G., & Spencer, D. L. (2005). Comparison of the educational deficiencies of delinquent and nondelinquent students. *Evaluation Review*, 29, 291–312. doi:10.1177/0193841X05275389

Watts-English, T., Fortson, B., Gibler, N., Hooper, S., & DeBellis, M. (2006). The psychobiology of maltreatment in childhood. *Journal of Social Issues*, *62*(4), 717–736. doi:10.1111/j.1540-4560.2006.00484.x

Weaver, T., Madden, P., Charles, V., Stimson, G., Renton, A., Tyrer, P., ... Ford, C. (2003). Comorbidity of substance misuse and mental illness in community mental health and substance misuse services. *The British Journal of Psychiatry*, *183*(4), 304–313. doi:10.1192/bjp.183.4.304

Welsh, B. C., Loeber, R., Stevens, B. R., Stouthamer-Loeber, M., Cohen, M. A., & Farrington, D. P. (2008). The costs of juvenile crime in urban areas: A longitudinal perspective. *Youth Violence and Juvenile Justice*, *6*, 3–27. doi:10.1177/1541204007308427

Wolff, K. T., Baglivio, M. T., & Piquero, A. R. (2015). The relationship between adverse childhood experiences and recidivism in a sample of juvenile offenders in community-based treatment. *International Journal of Offender Therapy and Comparative Criminology*, *49*, 1–33. doi:10.1177/0306624X15613992

Yu, R., Geddes, J. R., & Fazel, S. (2012). Personality disorders, violence, and antisocial behavior: A systematic review and meta-regression analysis. *Journal of Personality Disorders*, *26*(5), 775–792. doi:10.1521/pedi.2012.26.5.775

APPENDIX

THE PORTUGUESE STUDY ON DELINQUENCY AND SOCIAL MARGINALIZATION: SCIENTIFIC OUTCOMES

Doctoral thesis

Basto-Pereira, M. (2017). *Criminal persistence and psychosocial problems in young adults with a history of juvenile delinquency*. Unpublished doctoral thesis. University of Minho, Braga, Portugal.

Articles

Basto-Pereira, M., Começanha, R., Ribeiro, S., & Maia, A. (2015). Long-term predictors of crime desistance in juvenile delinquents: A systematic review of longitudinal studies. *Aggression and Violent Behavior, A Review Journal*, *25*(B), 332–342. doi:10.1016/j.avb.2015.09.012.

Basto-Pereira, M., Miranda, A., Ribeiro, S., & Maia, A. (2016). Growing up with adversity: From juvenile justice involvement, to criminal persistence and psychosocial problems in young adulthood. *Child Abuse and Neglect*, *62*, 63–75. doi:10.1016/j.chiabu.2016.10.011.

Basto-Pereira, M., Ribeiro, S., & Maia, A. (2017). Needs and achievements of the juvenile justice system: Insights from two empirical studies with Portuguese young adults. *International Journal of Offender Therapy and Comparative Criminology*. Advance online publication. doi:10.1177/0306624X17690450.

Basto-Pereira, M. & Maia, A. (2017a). *Early adversity and adult delinquency: The mediational role of mental health in youth offenders*. Manuscript submitted.

Basto-Pereira, M., & Maia, A. (2017b). *Persistence in crime in young adults with a history of juvenile delinquency: The role of mental health and psychosocial problems*. Manuscript submitted.

Conferences

Basto-Pereira, M, Farrington, D., & Maia, A. (2017, January). Delinquência Juvenil, marginalização social e carreira criminal [Juvenile Delinquency, Social Marginalization and Criminal Careers]. Paper presented at Congresso Nacional de Psicologia Forense [National Congress of Forensic Psychology], Lisboa, Portugal.

Basto-Pereira, M., Começanha, R., Ribeiro, S., & Maia, A. (2015, September). Long-term predictors of crime desistance in juvenile delinquents: A systematic review of longitudinal studies. Paper presented at 15th Annual Conference of the European Society of Criminology, Porto, Portugal.

Basto-Pereira, M., Miranda, A., Ribeiro, S., & Maia, A. (2016, May). Growing up with adversity: From juvenile justice involvement to criminal persistence and psychosocial problems in young adulthood. Paper presented at 5th Annual Conference of the European Association for Forensic Child & Adolescent Psychiatry, Psychology & other involved professions, Porto, Portugal.

Basto-Pereira, M., Ribeiro, S., & Maia, A. (2016, May). Needs and achievements of juvenile justice system: Insights from two matched control-studies. Poster session presented at 5th Annual Conference of the European Association for Forensic Child & Adolescent Psychiatry, Psychology & other involved professions, Porto, Portugal.

OTHER OUTCOMES RELATED TO PSDSM

Outcomes from the same research team, using the same sample and/or the same protocol used in the PSDSM:

Articles

Ribeiro, S., Basto-Pereira, M., & Maia, A. (2016). Intergenerational impact of mental illness in juveniles with history of victimization. *Psicologia, Saúde & Doenças*, *17*(1), 74–81. doi:10.15309/16psd170111.

Chapters

Basto-Pereira, M., Miranda, A., Ribeiro, S., & Maia, A. (in press). The psychometric properties of a questionnaire for measuring delinquency and crime (D-CRIM). In n/a (Ed.), *Avances en Psicología Clínica, 2015*. Granada, Espanã: Asociación Española de Psicología Conductual.

Master's thesis

Miranda, A. (2015). Fatores preditores do comportamento delinquente em jovens adultos da comunidade portuguesa [Predictors of delinquent behavior in young adults in the Portuguese community]. Tese de mestrado não publicada/ Unpublished master's thesis. Escola de Psicologia da Universidade do Minho, Lisboa, Portugal.

Ribeiro, S. (2015). Comportamento delinquente em jovens com vitimação autorreportada e em registo oficial [Delinquent behavior in youths with self-report and official records of victimization]. Tese de mestrado não publicada/ Unpublished master's thesis. Escola de Psicologia da Universidade do Minho, Lisboa, Portugal.

Conferences

Basto-Pereira, M., Miranda, A., Ribeiro, S., & Maia, A. (2015, November). The psychometric properties of a questionnaire for measuring delinquency and crime (D-CRIM). Poster session presented at VIII Congresso Internacional e XIII Nacional de Psicologia Clínica, Granada, Spain.

Maia, A., Miranda, A., Basto-Pereira, M., & Ribeiro, S. (2015, September). Pathways between childhood victimization and cognitive distortions associated with future criminal behavior. Paper presented at 15th Annual Conference of the European Society of Criminology, Porto.

Ribeiro, S., Basto-Pereira, M., & Maia, A. (2016, January). Impacto intergeracional da perturbação mental em jovens com história de vitimação [Intergenerational impact of mental illness in juveniles with history of victimization]. Paper presented at 11th Congresso Nacional de Psicologia da Saúde [National Congress of Health Psychology], Lisboa.

ABOUT THE AUTHORS

Miguel Basto Pereira has a PhD in Applied Psychology from University of Minho, Portugal. In addition, he has a Master's Degree in Statistics and a Master's Degree in Psychology. His doctoral research focused on: "Criminal persistence and psychosocial problems in young adults with a history of juvenile delinquency". His research interests include the links between childhood adversity and antisocial behavior; juvenile delinquent pathways; and, factors promoting desistance from crime and social insertion. Currently, his major topic of research is the study of lifelong crime sequences, a topic that this author advanced during his stay in University of Cambridge, as visiting doctoral student. Dr. Basto-Pereira's publications apply his scientific findings into policies that reduce or prevent crime and social marginalization. His research is published in some of the best journals in their field (e.g., *Aggression and Violent Behavior, Child Abuse & Neglect*). Miguel Basto Pereira is a lecturer in the Higher Institute for Applied Psychology (ISPA), which is the oldest Higher Education Institution Teaching Psychology in Portugal.

Ângela da Costa Maia is lecturer in the Applied Psychology Department, Vice President of the School of Psychology, and coordinates the Research Unit on Victims, Offenders and the Justice System in the University of Minho, Portugal. She is member of the board of the International Society of Behavioral Medicine, member of the Scientific Council of Stress Resource Center of the Ministry of Defense, and coordinates projects funded by the Foundation of Science and Technology, the Ministry of Internal Affairs, the Ministry of Health, and the Ministry of Defense. She is interested in understanding the impact of exposure to adversity, potentially traumatic experiences and associated factors, as well as pathways from victimization to delinquency. Her research is published in some of the best journals in their field.

INDEX

Printed and bound by CPI Group (UK) Ltd, Croydon, CR0 4YY

27/11/2025

14780749-0002